331.44
R

5/00
Du

THERE'S NO PLACE LIKE WORK

THERE'S NO PLACE LIKE WORK

*How Business, Government, and Our Obsession with Work
Have Driven Parents from Home*

BRIAN C. ROBERTSON

SPENCE PUBLISHING COMPANY • DALLAS

2000

To Mom and Dad,
who made 7707 Jervis Street home,
and to Matri Pulchrae Dilectionis—
help us put our families first.

Published in the United States by
Spence Publishing Company
111 Cole Street
Dallas, Texas 75207

Library of Congress Cataloging-in-Publication Data

Robertson, Brian C., 1964-
    There's no place like work : how business, government, and our obsession with work have driven parents from home / Brian C. Robertson.
        p. cm.
    Includes bibliographical references and index.
    ISBN 1-890626-18-x (hardcover)
        1. Working mothers—United States—Psychology.   2. Children of working parents—United States.   3. Work and family—Government policy—United States.   I. Title.
    HQ759.48 .R625   2000
    331.4'4'0973—dc21   99-046792

Printed in the United States of America

Contents

v

Introduction

First of all, let me be clear about what this book is not.

It does not pretend to be a scientifically objective study of sociological surveys, statistical trends, and polling data that—when carefully analyzed—inexorably lead to a conclusion that happens to correspond perfectly to the author's thesis. Surveys and sociological data can be useful to illustrate a point—and I use them throughout the text. But when authors hide behind statistics and references to convince the reader of their passionless objectivity, the reader who shares the modern credulity toward what is termed "social science" may be deceived. Sociological data are only as objective as the sociologist or pollster who did the original work, and an author usually has reasons to prefer some sources to others. The truth is that sociologists, reporters, and pollsters have viewpoints and presuppositions just as authors do.

I have gone beyond the mere citation of polling data and sociological studies and have entered—of necessity, I believe—into the realm of historical interpretation. The strength of social analysis does not lie in claims to scientific objectivity, but in compelling logic and the conformity of the argument to the experience and understanding of those who read it. Everyone brings a viewpoint to the debate over work and family—as to any matter related to human beings and how they shall order their familial and social relations—and those who claim that they do not are either deluded or disingenuous. In his classic book *Society and Sanity*, the late Frank Sheed insisted that all disputes about how society should be ordered presume some view of man, and the advisability of policy prescriptions touching on social issues ultimately depends on their conformity to man's nature.[1] This will be important to keep in mind as the battle over the culture—and the central cultural issue of how we choose to raise our children—continues in the coming years. The politics of the next decade will, I believe, be largely taken up with the question of whether parental care of children in the two-parent home is, or is not, an indispensable social norm. Radical experiments in family arrangements, particularly in the area of child rearing, are much more likely to be advocated by those who believe family roles to be purely conventional and infinitely malleable.

A textbook example of how the "science" of sociology is used in the service of political and ideological agendas occurred early in 1999 with the release of a study analyzing the effects of maternal employment on child development.[2] Immediately upon its publication in the *Journal of the American Psychological Association*, the study was given prominent coverage in the major news media. The study found, it was reported, that there are no detrimental effects on children from their mothers' employment outside the home. Typical of the coverage was a story on the *CBS Evening News* which began, "A new study shows children of women who work outside the home do just as well as those with stay at home moms."[3] Other headlines echoed that rosy assessment: the *Washington Post* proclaimed "Mothers' Employment Works for Children"[4]; the *Boston Globe* announced "Study says working mothers don't cause children harm"[5]; the *Atlanta Journal and Constitution* bannered "Working Moms Not Shortchanging Kids, Study Suggests."[6] The clear implication was that the study put to rest the antiquated notion that there are reasons for mothers to stay at home to take care of their young children: nonmaternal care works just as well, if not better.

In fact, the study showed nothing of the sort. Its author, Dr. Elizabeth Harvey of the University of Connecticut, had used data heavily skewed toward mothers who were young, poor, ill-educated, and members of minority groups. Compared with the general population, the mothers involved in the study were twice as likely to be black or Hispanic and twice as likely to be single mothers, their family income was less than half the national norm, and they were significantly below average in intelligence.[7] As several commentators later pointed out, many of the children in the sample may already have been "at risk" for performing poorly on cognitive and behavioral tests because of emotional, social, and economic deprivation. If anything, a finding of "no difference," in such a cross-section of the population, between the children of mothers who work and those of mothers who stay at home reveals that some of the negative effects of maternal employment on children may be diminished in a deprived family context, something Harvey herself acknowledged.[8]

Clearly, the findings could not be applied to American society as a whole—yet this is precisely what was claimed in the news stories. The *Boston Globe* even went so far as to headline its story "Working Moms Don't Spoil the Child With Day Care"—despite the fact that the *type* of alternative care provided in the mother's absence did not enter into the study at all.[9] Dr. Harvey herself did not seem worried about the media's seizing on her findings to endorse the increasingly frequent decision of mothers with young children to return to work. "Working mothers have a lot of guilt," Harvey opined, adding her hope that the study would "alleviate some of that guilt."[10]

Dr. Harvey's methodology gave no way of measuring whether the lack of negative effects among the group studied was related to the alternative care provided by commercial day care, other family members, or the fathers of the children in question. It was evident that the study had been taken up by journalistic advocates of uninterrupted careers for mothers of young children, whose agenda—as we will discover—includes preferential treatment for parents who choose the option of commercial child care over raising children at home. Her scientific objectivity was made more doubtful still by the questions raised about her methodology. The Statistical Assessment Service reported that Harvey "lowered the bar" for what differences in results among the children tested counted as "statistically significant"— which meant that it was not at all clear that her findings contradicted earlier studies that *did* find negative effects resulting from maternal employment. Her lumping together of mothers who worked only a few hours each week with those who worked up to forty hours would appear to have made it impossible to draw any general conclusions about the effects of maternal employment.[11]

In addition, the psychological tests employed in the study have no accurate way of measuring such vital but intangible aspects of children's well-being as feelings of loneliness, the sense of being wanted, the capacity to love, the ability to commit, or moral strength. And since the study looked only at children between the ages of three and twelve, developmental problems which manifest themselves later in the turbulent years of adolescence—when parents will tell you that maladjustments resulting from upbringing most often appear—were hidden from view.[12]

The lesson we should learn from the Harvey study and the media's reaction to it is not that sociological research is worthless, but that it can be—and often is—used selectively in the debate over what type of culture we shall have. In that continuing dispute, there is no more vexed or controversial issue than work and family, how the two interrelate, and what should be done about conflicting obligations and loyalties. What was most notable about the Harvey study episode was not the ambiguous and limited results of the study, but that they received such fervent attention from press and public alike. Detailed and technical sociological reports are not usually accorded front-page coverage by the major media, but when the emotional matter of work and family balance is being discussed, there is a much higher than normal level of public interest in what sociological research data might have to tell us about the results of our great experiment in reordering traditional professional and domestic arrangements.

The study received a remarkable amount of attention, Danielle Crittenden observed, because the findings appeared to absolve the typical dual-income, Yuppie family of the 1990s of guilt in the upbringing of their children. She wondered how data making the opposite case would be received: "Would a study purporting to show that small children suffered 'significant harm' when their mothers worked full-time be heralded by major media as vindication for mothers who stay home? Would networks lead their nightly news with the proclamation that mothers who put their children before their career needn't feel 'guilty' about not contributing to their household expenses or the gross national product?" Crittenden concluded that as an effort to alleviate the guilt of working moms, the study was likely to have precisely the opposite effect: "When the media join hands to celebrate a study that purports to show [a mother's] feelings are unfounded, it only exacerbates the feelings of guilt. A woman looking for ways to duck out of or minimize her time in the workforce, trying to convince her colleagues, her boss, and (often most difficult of all) her husband that she is needed by her child and that her role as a mother is a valuable and worthy one—the last thing she needs is to hear a cheerful chorus from all sides pronouncing that 'experts disagree.'"[13]

It is striking that despite the assurances of the media and the sociological "experts" that children have not been negatively affected by a vast shift of time and attention from home to work, there remains a strong sense among the public that something is deeply wrong with the parent-child relationship of the 1990s and that professional obligations are preventing people from giving their children the attention they need. The popular sense seems to be that children are not faring well in our society and that the decline in children's well-being is related to changes in the way children are brought up. An NBC-*Wall Street Journal* poll in 1999 showed a striking 83 percent of Americans agree that "parents not paying enough attention to what's going on in their childrens' lives" has become a "very serious problem." An entire industry of "experts" has arisen in recent years to debunk "myths" about child rearing that most people take as obviously true (such as the strange idea that mothers raise their own children better than anyone else does).

An illustration of this imperviousness to expert assurances that all is well with our increasing reliance as a society on nonparental child care was the reaction to Littleton. In April 1999, two high school boys massacred thirteen of their classmates at a public high school in affluent Littleton, Colorado, before taking their own lives. With little information about the family situations of either of the boys involved, there was an almost instinctive gravitation toward the notion that the tragedy was related to endemic parental neglect of children in a work-obsessed, money-driven culture. Interestingly, this notion was heard not just from cultural conservatives, but also from those most friendly to the cultural changes represented by the movement of mothers into the workplace over the course of the last generation. In a commencement address at Grambling State University in Louisiana, President Clinton spoke at length about the issue of work-family balance in the context of the events at Littleton. "In the aftermath of the terrible tragedy at Littleton and the other school shootings we've had in our country," said the president, "they've forced us to confront the need not only to make guns less available to criminals and children, not only to make our culture less violent and our schools safer, but also to make the bonds that tie parents to children stronger." Clinton used the opportunity to announce the institution of new, expanded family leave policies for federal workers, which he put forth as a model for private employers, and to propose several new policy initiatives to address the issue of work-family balance.[14]

There is no question that the issue of work-family balance will be on everyone's political agenda in coming years, the only question being what policies—based on what principles—will be enacted. President Clinton advocates going further in the direction of subsidizing dual-income families who choose commercial day care, with his stated aim of "more affordable, higher quality child care" for working parents. Since the trend of mothers toward the workplace is both inevitable and irreversible, on his view, government must help to ease the burdens of working parents, both by subsidizing the personal choice of day care and mandating employer flexibility, particularly in leave policies. Republicans, however, favor reforming labor law to allow more scheduling flexibility on the part of working parents, weakening laws that regulate overtime work.[15]

It is the burden of this book to show that both of these are simplistic, quick-fix approaches, and are dangerous to the extent that they ignore the policy sources of the economic and social pressures that have led to the American flight from domesticity over the past thirty years. They demean those families that continue to make considerable economic and professional sacrifices so that one parent may stay home, and they affront the majority of working mothers who feel that they have little choice whether to work.

So let me state at the beginning that I come to the subject of work and family with the definite impression that too many Americans are neglecting their family obligations as a result of the pressure—both self-imposed and from their employers—to spend more time at work, an impression I find to be supported by a reasonable analysis of available data. The interesting question, explored in the pages that follow, is not whether this flight from the home is occurring, but why.

That question has not been given much attention in the voluminous commentary and analysis given to the issue of "balancing" work and family obligations. All too often, in what has been written on the subject, there seems to be an attempt to grapple with the "problem" of conflicting loyalties and obligations at work and at home, without any preliminary investigation of how this dilemma came about in the first place. The assumption, in many cases, seems to be that the movement toward the workplace—especially in the case of mothers—has been an inevitable historical development and that the most we can do is to come up with stopgap measures to address some of its more egregious consequences: the neglect of children in their preschool years; the psychological, emotional, and family strain incurred by the increasing number of people in our society who find themselves unable to fulfill their obligations at home and work. The reason for this failure to examine the historical and cultural background of the changes in our thinking about work and family is clear: it is a complex task to trace all the contributions to the dramatic changes in our view of home and work. But to avoid this complex task is to adopt an extremely shallow and ultimately reductionist view of the matter, which leads to apparent solutions (such as government-mandated flexible-work and family-leave policies on the part of employers and more subsidization of commercial day care) that at best address only the symptoms of the larger cultural crisis and at worst aggravate it.

I have chosen a different approach. Since it is vital to appreciate rightly the cultural, economic, and political changes that have led us where we are, this book looks at the history of the evolution in our attitudes as a society on questions of work and home, and at how that evolution in attitudes has affected family policy in this country. I begin in chapter one by noting that while there has been a developing consensus over the past decade about the detrimental effects of divorce and illegitimacy on children, no consensus, as yet, exists about the effects of the declining amount of time parents are spending with their children and the resulting phenomenon of surrogate parenting. This reluctance to face up to the accumulating data pointing to the detrimental effects of parental neglect and surrogate parenting on children is itself, I argue, perhaps the supreme manifestation of the cultural revolution that has made full-time maternal care of children the exception rather than the rule. In the following chapter, I take a look at the prevailing attitudes toward home and motherhood earlier in this century and find that some of the most vigorous advocates of the idea that mothers should not be forced to neglect their child-rearing responsibilities because of economic necessity were to be found in the socially progressive women's movement.

Chapter two takes up the change in attitudes about motherhood and the domestic realm that was part of the dramatic shift in the thinking of the women's movement on the subject, a change of much more recent vintage than one might expect. Along with this change in thinking about the domestic realm (and the responsibilities intrinsically connected to that realm) came a change in the way our culture regards the place and purpose of work. This history is explored in chapter three. The change in thinking about home and work documented in these two chapters, of course, was related to the prevailing economic and corporate environment—particularly regarding the choices which that environment encourages and discourages. This relation is explored in chapter four. The economic developments that have created (or failed to create) an environment conducive to family and domestic commitments have not been entirely random; on the contrary, they are a result of policies consciously pursued—either heedless of their effect on families or intentionally sapping the vitality of the domestic realm. This history is traced in chapter five, which also contains a brief sketch of family policies that may help to reinvigorate family life. Finally, chapter six surveys promising developments that point out the direction in which we will have to consciously direct our personal and collective energies if we wish to attain a sustainable social equilibrium that gives proper value to both the professional and domestic realms.

Although at times anecdotal in style, this is not a "how to" book that, in gnostic fashion, claims to reveal the hidden key to "success" for a society obsessed with quick, tangible results. I pretend to no such secret knowledge, but merely present my own analysis of the movement away from the home and toward the workplace as the center of social activity. Only when we perceive this trend properly—judging rightly its scope, causes, and effects in society—can we hope to arrive at even a provisional solution.

Success is a relative concept, and one of the questions I intend to examine is whether it might be necessary in the current environment to sacrifice some measure of financial success and career advancement in order to succeed as parents, spouses, neighbors, and responsible citizens. Perhaps that will prove the only way to change the environment.

Finally, this book is not a personal testimony. Like most in our society, I have grappled with balancing work and family obligations— with varying degrees of success. While my own experience has given me some insights, there are many who are better equipped than I to speak to the question of how to be competent and respected professionals while at the same time partaking fully of the joys and responsibilities that come with family life. Some of them speak in this book.

There seems to be a growing recognition that something is wrong with our whole concept of work—its purpose and meaning—as well as a growing dissatisfaction with the way the demands of the workplace increasingly pull people away from their obligations at home. It is clear that no resolution of this apparent conflict will be forthcoming until enough of us can at least vaguely envision an alternative to the status quo—a society where work and family, far from being at odds, are mutually beneficial aspects of an integrated, satisfying existence. Only when we have seen the ideal to be striven for can we move toward it.

I OWE SPECIAL THANKS to Mrs. Kennedy-Smith, at whose home the general outline of this book was forged; to Luis Tellez and the folks at Mercer for their hospitality for a crucial two weeks; to Patrick Fagan, John Mueller, and Alvaro DeVicnente for reviewing and critiquing early drafts; to Allan Carlson for his scholarship and encouragement; to David Jessup for his support and patience; to Michael Devine for his hard work in helping me to bring the project to completion; to my editor Mitchell Muncy for his helpful suggestions and guidance; and to my brothers for putting up with me during the time it took to get it done.

THERE'S NO PLACE LIKE WORK

The Real *Child Care Crisis*

*The lack of good quality, affordable child care is a
silent crisis. We want American parents to succeed
at the most important task they have: caring for the
next generation and being good workers.*

—Hillary Rodham Clinton

OVER THE PAST TEN YEARS, an astonishing new consensus has developed, one that would have been difficult—if not impossible—to foresee at the beginning of the decade. It has become increasingly clear that disapproval of illegitimacy and divorce—including disapproval of the single-parent family that results from those behaviors—is slowly but surely being restored.

That some measure of our society's traditional censure of having children out of wedlock and of casually dissolving the bonds of marriage is returning will be apparent from a glance at a few cultural indicators. After the convulsions of the 1960s, it became fashionable among academics and intellectuals to sing the praises of "family diversity"—to assert that the traditional family structure of husband, wife, and children living under the same roof is antiquated and arbitrary and that the "nuclear family" is based on nothing more than Western cultural biases left over from an outmoded patriarchy. Indicative of the prevailing mood was the hostile reaction to "The Negro Family: The Case for National Action," a 1965 policy report written by Assistant Secretary of Labor Daniel Patrick Moynihan. Moynihan called the rising rate of illegitimacy in the black community—then 25 percent—a national crisis that demanded immediate action, and he concluded that the chief threat to the continued economic and social advancement of blacks was the breakdown of the traditional family within the black community.[1] For suggesting that the growing number of female-headed households in the black community was cause for concern, Moynihan was widely vilified as a racist attempting to impose traditional white-European family structures on minority populations, and his report was denounced as an exercise in blaming the victim. The Johnson Administration, cowed by the harsh response of many black political leaders, quietly buried the report.[2]

A new spirit was then in the ascendancy in the popular culture—the desire for individual sexual and ethical liberation from traditional societal restraints. It was not, of course, just among black political leaders that this ethic prevailed. The zeal to abandon old, outworn cultural norms—particularly those relating to marriage, family, and sexual morality—held sway throughout the cultural establishment of the era, both among the entertainment and news media and in supposedly more serious academic circles. According to these advocates of "family diversity," nothing prevented our society from welcoming a wide variety of domestic arrangements: cohabitation before (or instead of) marriage, homosexual partnerships, single motherhood (whether from sexual choices freely made or from divorce), and adoption of children into any one of these diverse forms of "family"—all were declared to be valid options based solely on one's personal preference. In the sexually liberated future, the two-parent family would be exposed as an irrational constraint on individual fulfillment, which had resulted in a repressed, bigoted, and conformist culture that had maintained itself only by punishing those who deviated from cultural norms.

As the radical theories of the 1960s became the tenured ortho-doxy of the 1970s and 1980s, it became increasingly difficult—if not positively dangerous—in academic circles even to question the pre-vailing orthodoxy of family diversity. This was especially true in the thoroughly radicalized discipline of sociology. "It was absolutely *ver-boten*," says David Popenoe, a prestigious sociologist who now teaches at Rutgers University. "You simply could not bring it up, because the dominant ideology viewed the traditional family as something that one was well rid of." Despite—or perhaps because of—this taboo, Popenoe began to study the matter. His 1988 book, *Disturbing the Nest: Family Change and Decline in Modern Societies*, "blew the whistle," says Popenoe, on the effects of divorce and illegitimacy on children. A social scientist of impeccably progressive credentials— some of whose urban planning research in the mid-1960s had a di-rect influence on the social welfare programs of the Great Society— Popenoe could not easily be dismissed as a traditionalist crank pin-ing for the days of the Ozzie-and-Harriet-style American family of the 1950s. The book meticulously documented numerous adverse effects on the nation's children of the breakdown of the two-parent family, and its message is being amplified today in the social science community, in the mainstream press, and even in our popular and political discourse.[3]

An early indicator of the new respectability of defending the norm of the two-parent family came when Vice President Dan Quayle, in 1992, criticized the popular sitcom *Murphy Brown* for glorifying the choice to have a child out of wedlock. Predictably, Quayle was mocked by the news and entertainment industries and was accused of attacking single mothers, who are the victims, said his critics, of an unfair wage system that favors men. For publicly addressing the breakdown of the two-parent family Quayle was called intolerant and hidebound—a reactionary who was resisting inevitable economic and social change. Republican strategists dropped the issue for the rest of the presidential campaign, convinced that the topic was too divisive to exploit politically with an electorate heavily populated with single mothers.

But the pillorying of Quayle for daring to question the reigning orthodoxy of family diversity soon ended. In 1993, social historian Barbara Dafoe Whitehead, in a remarkable article in the *Atlantic Monthly* entitled "Dan Quayle Was Right," laid out the case that all is not well in the brave new world of alternative family structures. Whitehead argued that as the facts have accumulated on children of divorced and single parents, it has become apparent that, according to nearly every standard, they fare significantly worse than their peers in two-parent families. Children in single-parent families, for instance, are six times more likely to be poor and three times more likely to have emotional or behavioral problems; their rates of teenage pregnancy and drug abuse are much higher; and they are far more likely to drop out of high school. Nor do the negative effects of one-parent households end with childhood. Whitehead pointed to data clearly indicating that children from single-parent homes have a more difficult time achieving intimacy in a relationship and in forming a stable marriage themselves. They even have more trouble holding a steady job. Surprisingly, the statistics are just as bad or worse for children whose parents remarry after divorce; only the presence of their two biological parents seems to provide the stability most children need during their formative years.

The results of our "vast experiment in family life," according to Whitehead, were clear for all to see: "dissolution of two-parent families ... is harmful to many children, and dramatically undermines our society."[4] Whitehead's article marked the beginning of a new phase in our public discourse on families, a phase in which it is no longer dangerous to speak of traditional family structures as preferable—at least when one is discussing the interests of children. Only a year after Quayle was ridiculed for criticizing single motherhood, President Clinton stated that he, too, believed that the former vice president had been right. Even actress Candice Bergen, who played Murphy Brown on the television series, recently admitted that Quayle's remarks had been on target.[5] Today, it is common to see articles and editorials in the major media that point out the detrimental effects that divorce and illegitimacy have on children, and even suggest various remedial measures. All this would have been inconceivable ten years ago.

On our nation's campuses, however, there is continued resistance to those who would question the notion of family diversity, a resistance arising mainly from the ideological dominance of feminism. "There is still prevalent in the world of academia, sociology in particular, the view that to say 'two-parent families are better' is controversial," according to Popenoe. "It's viewed as an attack on feminism, because one of the biggest changes in the last thirty years has been the influx of women into the workplace. If you even use the word *decline* to describe what's happening, everybody's furious, because it implies somehow that the whole movement of women to the workplace was a terrible mistake, and that they ought to all go back home."[6] Feminist thinkers are now the primary champions of the view that the nuclear family is an artificial construct specific to Western societies and that the decline of the two-parent family is both inevitable and desirable. Stephanie Coontz, in her 1993 book *The Way We Never Were: American Families and the Nostalgia Trap*, declared that women's new sexual freedom and increased economic independence has exploded the old, outmoded definitions of family. Coontz and other feminists argue that Americans should celebrate this new diversity. In modern society, they argue, any mutually beneficial living arrangement can and should be considered a viable family. As for the data indicating significant barriers to children's development associated with growing up in a single-parent home, these are said to come from the unfair social stigma still attached to divorce and illegitimacy and from government policies that lag behind social reality. Instead of further stigmatizing "nontraditional" families, public policy should mitigate the adverse economic effects of divorce and single parenthood, in part by reducing unemployment and encouraging pay equity, in part by favoring the revising of work schedules and by knocking down barriers that keep women from reaching high-level executive positions.[7]

The response of such feminist academics to the considerable body of evidence that documents the numerous ways in which children suffer from illegitimacy and divorce is certainly inadequate (since it consists largely of ideological assertion rather than an attempt to refute the data). But the focus of their argument indicates they are more accurate in their assessment of what is at stake than are Popenoe and his colleagues, who insist that their concern with the breakdown of traditional family structure is compatible with a generally feminist worldview. For Coontz and other feminists recognize that in identifying illegitimacy and divorce as social pathologies that must be fought, the developing consensus undermines a fundamental premise of modern American feminism: that women should be completely independent in both the economic and the reproductive realms. That "independence" is expressed in the large-scale entry of mothers with young children into the workforce over the past thirty years. If the doctrine that family structure is infinitely malleable can be successfully challenged, we will be well on the way toward asserting that women have—and will continue to have—primary responsibility for child care. And if the bad effects of illegitimacy and divorce can be shown to come, in some measure, from the attempt of single parents to combine child-rearing and breadwinning responsibilities (an attempt that results in the neglect of children during their formative years), then doubt will be cast on the wisdom of our "vast social experiment" which has seen the mass movement of mothers with preschool children into the labor force, an experiment that has been much more drastic among *married* women than among single or divorced women.

THE LATCH-KEY CULTURE

All indications are that the social pathologies resulting from single-parent homes, as described by Popenoe and Whitehead, are directly related to the decrease in the time that parents spend with children during the formative years. "Family disruption creates a deep division between parents' interests and the interests of children," writes Whitehead. "One of the worst consequences of these divided interests is a withdrawal of parental investment in children's well-being."[8] A prominent manifestation, among many, of parents' disinvestment in their children's welfare is the sharp decrease in the amount of time they spend together. By one estimate, the number of "latch-key" children unattended at home for much of the day after school, rose from 1.6 million in 1976 to twelve million in 1994.[9] On average, according to another recent study, parents today spend only seventeen hours per week with their children, about 43 percent fewer hours than in 1965.[10] Noting that this has occurred despite the fact that there are "far fewer children per family today as compared with the Baby Boom period," Harvard professor Richard Gill, in *Posterity Lost*, calls it "a dramatic, history-shattering development, and the only question is whether there is any other possible explanation except the blatantly obvious one, namely, that the interests of children today are being given a much lower priority as compared with the interests of their parents."[11]

One might be tempted to accuse Gill of hyperbole had he not documented the assertion earlier in the book with a list of dismaying signs that point to a crisis of child neglect in the United States: rates of infant mortality, child abuse, children in poverty, teen suicide, drug abuse, and high school dropouts all show an increase between 1970 and 1994 that Gill calls "stunning." During the same period, youth homicide and crime rates soared—even in years when the rates for adults were declining. SAT scores plummeted to the point where American children are at or near the bottom when ranked against other industrialized nations. As for reckless sexual activity, "despite AIDS and other sexually transmitted diseases," writes Gill, "sexual intercourse is occurring earlier and earlier among American young people, increasingly with multiple partners."[12] When Senator Moynihan, twenty years after his warning about the breakdown of the black family, said that "the United States may be the first society in history in which children are distinctly worse off than adults,"[13] he was not referring only to material poverty.

While it would be impossible—as well as unwise—to assert that all of these signs of the declining well-being of children are attributable solely to the shrinking amount of time that parents devote to their children, the social science data indicating a definite relationship are substantial. A 1995 study of adolescent sexual activity showed that first sexual experimentation most often occurs at home in the parents' absence, concluding "it appears that an empty and unsupervised home provides more opportunity for the adolescent as well as for the younger grade-school latch-key child to engage in sex."[14] With regard to teenage suicide, a 1986 survey of high school students showed that in the estimation of those respondents who knew a classmate who had committed or attempted suicide, the major causes included "a feeling of personal worthlessness," deriving from "a feeling of isolation and loneliness."[15] After it was learned that the teenage killers in Littleton had made and stored bombs in their parents' homes, many immediately wondered whether closer parental supervision could have prevented the tragedy.

Another recent study in a prominent sociological journal documented a link between poor academic performance and a mother's professional commitment outside the home. In a 1994 volume of *Pediatric Annals*, physicians Elizabeth M. Aldeman and Stanford B. Friedman of Albert Einstein College of Medicine explained the surprisingly high incidence of sexual experimentation, drug use, and delinquency in teens from affluent families by saying that, on the basis of their study, "being home alone without supervision may predispose [adolescents] to these behaviors" because "their parents may be preoccupied socially or professionally, and may not make the necessary quality time for them at home."[16] Sociologist Mark Warr of the University of Texas confirmed this in another study which sought to correlate the time parents spend with children and the rate of juvenile delinquency. He concluded that "contemporary arguments notwithstanding, small amounts of quality time may not be sufficient to offset the criminogenic aspects of peer culture to which adolescents are commonly exposed."[17]

Other recent studies have attributed various mental illnesses in children—ranging from depression to "borderline psychopathology"—to lack of parental attention.[18] The recent rash of shootings in suburban public schools has led commentators and politicians to call for stricter gun control laws and less glamorization of violence in the entertainment industry. Less culturally acceptable—but more relevant since the availability of guns and the cultural obsession with violence have not changed considerably over the years—might be a call for stricter parental supervision of the cultural fare children are consuming, be it video games, movies, or music. This, however, would depend upon a fairly constant parental presence in the home, and that can no longer be taken for granted, or even posited as the norm.

The time deficit afflicting the child-parent relationship in the United States is an unstated yet clearly present theme in many analyses of social pathologies. For instance, the depiction of explicit sex and violence on television and its influence on children is much discussed, but few note that the increasing amount of unsupervised time children spend watching television is itself an indicator of the lack of parental attention. According to a 1990 study, children aged two to five spend an average of twenty-five hours a week watching television, "more time than performing any other activity except sleeping."[19] Although a 1995 *New York Times* poll showed that the explosion of teen violence and sex was attributed by Americans in equal measures to the influence of television and to family breakdown, a closer look at the poll reveals that many parents felt "powerless" to control their children's television watching precisely because they were "not around" to do so.[20]

The clearest indication that diminished parental attention is having a devastating effect on children is the alarm with which both parents and children themselves regard the phenomenon. A study published last year in the *Journal of the American Medical Association* concluded that teens who feel they are paid attention to by their parents are less likely to use drugs, drink alcohol, smoke, or have sex.[21] Another recent study showed that although half of the nation's youth watch television more than two hours a day, three-fourths of these children say that they would choose more time with their parents if they had the option.[22] A recent survey of sixth- through twelfth-graders showed that 20 percent had not had a conversation longer than ten minutes with either of their parents in more than a month.[23] Half of all parents, according to a 1995 Gallup poll, feel that they do not spend enough time with their children; for employed parents, the proportion is two-thirds. The same survey showed that only one-third of the respondents ate dinner with their children on a regular basis.[24] These self-incriminating responses are all the more extraordinary when one considers the subjective nature of such polls: it is unlikely, to say the least, that the parents polled are *under*estimating their own performance.

MOTHER-ABSENCE

While the problem of father-absence in broken families has recently been the subject of a good deal of commentary, the father is increasingly absent in intact families as well because of the steadily increasing pressure to spend more time in the office. (What accounts for this trend and whether the pressure is social, economic, employer- or self-imposed is a question that will be addressed later.) It is abundantly apparent, however, that the really revolutionary development over the past thirty years—and the one which accounts for most of the vanished time parents used spend with their children—is the astounding increase in the number of married mothers who work outside the home. Although the developing consensus on illegitimacy and divorce may have led to a new appreciation of the father's indispensable role in the emotional, behavioral, and character development of children, this makes the relative neglect in recent years of the *mother's* formative role all the more difficult to account for, particularly given that child-welfare advocates have historically emphasized the mother's indispensable role as primary caregiver. A good deal of the neglect, no doubt, derives from the reluctance (alluded to by David Popenoe) of many academics and opinion leaders to be seen as hostile to the social advancement of women, particularly in the realm of professional achievement. Some, including politicians and other public figures, do not take up the issue of maternal neglect for fear of alienating the large and growing number of working mothers in the electorate. But the fact remains that any serious attempt to grapple with the issue of decreasing parental time and attention devoted to children (and the subsequent declining formative influence of parents) must take up the issue of working mothers, as well as the closely related matter of whether alternative care arrangements for the children can ever be adequate substitutes for mother-care.

The statistics on the workforce participation of married mothers show that we are dealing with a social experiment of vast proportions, one at least as significant as the steep rises in the rates of illegitimacy and divorce over the same period, and one whose long-term effects can only be guessed at. According to the U.S. Bureau of Labor Statistics, the percentage of married mothers with dependent children under the age of eighteen who work full-time and year-round has increased dramatically in the past twenty-five years alone, rising from

20 percent in 1976 to 42 percent in 1997.[25] Broken down, the statistics show that almost half of married mothers with school-age children are now working full-time, and a full third of married mothers with preschool children work full-time. Unsurprisingly, this increase was about equal to the decline in the percentage of married mothers who stayed at home and did not engage in market work (devoting their full time to the care of children and other homemaking responsibilities): about 43 percent of married mothers were stay-at-home in 1976, but only 23 percent were in 1997.[26]

Just how sweeping the change in attitudes toward the responsibilities of motherhood has been is revealed when one compares the employment rates for married mothers to those of unmarried mothers over the same period. The percentage of unmarried mothers employed full-time in 1964 was twice that of married mothers (or about 20 percent); in 1996 it was still under 35 percent.[27] Another way of illustrating the point is that the percentage of married mothers who have preschool children and who are working full time now exceeds the same measure of unmarried mothers for the first time since statistics have been kept.[28] It would seem that we are now experiencing a strange dynamic in which married mothers feel more compulsion (or necessity) to support their dependent children than do unmarried mothers.

Women now make up almost exactly half of the professional workforce; in 1960 the figure was only 33 percent. That it is married women—and specifically married mothers—that account for this sharp increase is beyond question. The total percentage of *unmarried* women in the workforce has actually declined slightly in the past decade after having risen steadily between 1960 and 1986, whereas the percentage of married women who work keeps rising. Over this same period, the percentage of married *men* in the workforce has actually dropped, declining from 89 percent in 1960 to about 78 percent today.[29] Another surprising development is this: the percentage of married mothers who work now exceeds the total percentage of married women in the workforce, for the rate of increase has been much more gradual among married women who are childless than it has been among those who have kids at home. Not only is the number of mothers who return to the workforce after their children reach school age sharply up (an increase of 22 percent in the past twenty-five years alone), but the trend is *more* dramatic for mothers with preschool children. Between 1970 and 1996, the total percentage of married women in the workforce with children of preschool age rose from 44 percent to 68 percent, meaning that more than two-thirds of married mothers who have children under six years of age now engage in some professional work. This statistical reversal constitutes more than the death of sexual stereotypes or a change in cultural attitudes about gender roles; it represents a radical change in cultural attitudes toward motherhood and child rearing. The question we cannot avoid is whether anyone is making up for the time that mothers no longer spend with their children. If not, the question becomes even more difficult: namely, can anyone adequately make up for it?

The changing complexion of America's workforce and the issues it raises—pay equity, sexual discrimination and harassment, the female presence in traditionally male-dominated professions—have been the subject of an enormous amount of commentary, and the professional accomplishments of women in recent years are generally regarded with warm approval. A married mother is no longer seen as exclusively responsible for the work of caring for home and children, and a married man is no longer regarded only as a breadwinner, but each now shares some of the traditional role of the other. It is clear, however, that the time deficit in mother-care for children has not been made up for by a corresponding increase in the amount of time that married fathers invest in that vital activity. In fact married *fathers* are considerably more likely to work—both full- and part-time—than are married men without children: this is precisely the opposite of the dynamic that still prevails among married mothers, despite their continuing movement from the home to the office.[30] In addition, a recent study by psychologist William T. Bailey at Eastern Illinois University indicates that fathers who take on the primary child care role are actually less responsive to the needs of their children than those fathers who are less directly involved in caregiving.[31] Statistics also indicate that husbands working full-time whose wives do not work spend considerably more time, on average, with their children than do husbands with working wives, presumably because the mother at home makes more demands for his time and effort with the children.[32] The conclusion is as striking as it is disturbing: at a time when children's well-being has been declining according to every measure, their primary caregivers—married mothers with dependent children—account for most of the vast and historically unprecedented influx of women into the workforce, and married fathers have not discernibly made up for the diminishing maternal care.[33]

At the very least, this indicates the demise of the traditional view of marriage that long held sway in Western society. It was thought that one of the primary benefits of marriage is that it eliminates the need for mothers to perform both breadwinning and child-rearing roles, thus freeing them to devote their time and energies to the latter. The now-prevalent notion that professional work (and indeed career ambition) liberates women from the mundane and oppressive duties of motherhood and homemaking—rather than interfering with the fulfillment of those duties—is without precedent in the West.

Critics have pointed out, with some justification, that the figures on working moms can be misleading and are often used disingenuously by proponents of government-subsidized child care to promote their agenda.[34] Many supporters of increased government spending on child care programs do, in fact, use the statistics on working mothers to bolster their case that the dual-earner couple is now the norm and that policymakers must face the reality of the situation by helping families as they exist, not according to some antiquated model. One might easily get the impression from advocates of federal day care legislation—and most media coverage of the issue—that a full

68 percent of mothers with preschool children work outside the home full-time and would opt to put their children in high-quality day care centers if they had the option. The truth is quite different: a majority of that 68 percent works either part-time or at home, and for those who do opt for nonmaternal child care, putting their children in day care centers is far from the preferred arrangement. The number of children whose mothers work and who are cared for by family members, relatives, or neighbors is more than twice the number currently in day care centers.

That said, it is clear that the source of the enormous overall increase in the number of working mothers in the past twenty-five years has been the steep rise in those who have chosen to work full-time, year-round. Even more important, it actually *is* the case that the model of parents who both work full-time, year-round is today significantly more common than the traditional arrangement of the father who works full-time and the mother who stays at home to care for the kids and the domestic responsibilities. Since 1976 (when it was still by far the most common family type), the proportion of families with fathers working full time and mothers devoting their full time to home and family has been cut in half, from four in ten to about two in ten.[35] During the same period, the proportion of families with children in which both parents work full-time has gone from 25 percent to over 45 percent and is now more common than any other work pattern for families with children, significantly exceeding the number of those families where the father works full-time and the mother works part-time.[36] Even when one looks only at the work patterns of parents with children under six, *the proportion of those families in which both mother and father work full-time now exceeds that in which the mother is devoted exclusively to home and family.* Whether this has been the result of economic factors or of social pressures (or a combination of both) will be addressed later.

We have obviously experienced a major shift in our cultural paradigms with regard to work, the rearing of children, and domestic responsibilities, and those who do not wish to undermine further the shrinking number of families who still rear their own children at home—often at considerable personal cost—will not help those families by simply asserting that working mothers are already making arrangements that are quite adequate, without any help from the government.[37] As long as trends continue in the direction of more nonparental care of children—be it formal day care centers or more informal arrangements—there will be an increasing demand for the government to subsidize dual-earner families who use day care for their children. Those genuinely concerned about arresting (or even reversing) these trends—if only for the sake of improving our children's well-being—are going to have to use both public policy and cultural reinforcement to support women who devote themselves to caring for their own children.

ADEQUATE CARE?

The preliminary data from our massive social experiment in surrogate parenting are not at all encouraging. They provide more than enough reason to inquire seriously whether previous generations had a more realistic understanding of what kind of parental attention is entailed in the successful rearing of children, as well as the relationship that vitally important endeavor has to the maintenance of a healthy society.

For determining the adequacy of nonparental care of young children, one of the primary sources of evidence will be the growing system of day care centers across the country. The thriving commercial child care industry is on the cutting edge of our massive social experiment in alternative child rearing. While the percentage of married mothers with children of preschool age who opt for putting their children in organized child care facilities is still slightly less than that of those who choose informal day care arrangements outside the child's home, such as relatives or neighbors (29 percent vs. 31 percent), the proportion of those choosing day care has tripled since 1970, during the same period in which the number of working mothers exploded.[38] Of married mothers who work full-time, more than one third now use formal day care, as the percentage opting for informal care in another home also continues to decline steadily.[39] If trends continue in their present direction, in a short time organized day care facilities will be the most popular child care option for these working mothers.

This has particularly important implications for the preschool children, especially the infants, who are placed in these institutions. In this connection, the recent history of theories of child development is worth recounting. In the immediate postwar era, when use of formal day care was statistically negligible compared to today, "experts" held that babies need only minimal care in the first few years of their development; essentially nutrition, hygiene, and protection from physical harm. As for their mental and psychological development, the theory was that infants are passive, unable to seek out much from their surroundings. Perceived social responses are, according to one scientific curriculum, "a figment of the over-involved mother's imagination, since baby's behavior is random, uncontrolled, essentially autistic." Aside from that, it was said, discipline and behavioral conditioning are what is most needed for proper development, and these can be provided by any caregiver.[40]

Today, the old consensus among child development experts has been reversed. Researchers now assure us that babies are able to respond to and distinguish various stimuli from birth. More important, the evidence shows that newborn infants, almost immediately, establish a strong and irreplaceable relationship with their mother. Pediatricians Marshall Klaus and John Kennel put it succinctly: "Detailed studies of the amazing behavioral capacities of the normal neonate have shown that the infant sees, hears, and moves in rhythm to his mother's voice in the first minutes and hours of life."[41] Instead of seeing infants as "passive bundles," child behavior researchers now almost universally recognize that the minds of babies are surprisingly sophisticated.[42]

All of this recent research would seem to support "attachment" theories of early child development, long favored by those who maintain the irreducible importance of the mother-child bond. Attachment theory posits that the early relationship between young children and their parents is the foundation of *all* personality development. The security established in a stable, nurturing relationship with one person—presumably the mother—on whom the developing infant can depend unreservedly is, according to this theory, essential in establishing the sense of selfhood and identity necessary for subsequent character growth. This dependent relationship becomes, paradoxically, the basis for the child's future independence.[43]

"Without someone specifically oriented to his needs," wrote D. W. Winnicott, a psychoanalyst whose work has been an important source for much of attachment theory, "the infant cannot find a working relation to external reality. Without someone to give satisfactory instinctual gratifications, the infant cannot find his body, nor can he develop an integrated personality. Without one person to love and to hate, he cannot come to know that it is the same person that he loves and hates, and so cannot find his sense of guilt, and his desire to repair and restore."[44]

According to this thesis, if a child is deprived of this relationship, especially in the first two years, there will be lasting physical, cognitive, and emotional impairments. The logic of attachment theory leads to the conclusion that, in the words of the theory's original proponent, John Bowlby, "a home must be very bad before it is bettered by a good institution."[45]

In fact, Bowlby's research as far back as the 1940s tends to bear this out, little regarded though it was at the time. His studies of children who had undergone traumatic separations from their parents— many of them young evacuees from London during the German air raids—showed a consistent pattern of lasting emotional detachment and stunted development as a result of sustained periods of minimal maternal contact.[46]

The irreplaceable nature of maternal care in a child's early years was also attested by other, more surprising, sources. Anna Freud, daughter of the founder of modern psychoanalysis, set up the Hampstead Nurseries in London to care for the same class of children studied by Bowlby, those displaced by the German bombing. Her conclusions were much the same as Bowlby's. A world-renowned child analyst who believed strongly in the importance of early relationships, Freud chose the staff of the nurseries with care, and the practices instituted were based on the latest in child psychology. Still, in these controlled conditions—about as favorable as could be imagined—the children fared considerably worse by most measurements than those raised in average families. In speech skills, the average two-year-old at Hampstead was six months behind the average child of the same age looked after at home. Freud's wards were more aggressive and had less control of their impulses, were less cooperative, more listless, and later in achieving toilet training than their counterparts raised at home. Freud considered the nurseries definitive proof that there was no adequate substitute for maternal care.[47]

Dr. Benjamin Spock, the eminent child care authority often associated with the liberalization of attitudes concerning the rearing of children, was traditional when it came to substitutes for maternal care: "A day nursery . . . is no good for an infant. There's nowhere near enough attention or affection to go around."[48] Another unlikely proponent of attachment theory (before it had a name), sociologist Margaret Mead, was unambiguous: "A little baby needs continuity of care; all our studies suggest that too frequent changes of the mothering person are hard on children. . . . We do not know—man has never known—how else to give a human being a sense of selfhood and identity, a sense of the worth of the world."[49]

But perhaps the ultimate case study to test the validity of attachment theory occurred in much more recent times. Since the collapse of Communism in 1989, over eighteen thousand children from Romanian orphanages have been adopted by couples in the United States. Most of these children—deprived of their mothers from infancy—were confined to cribs much of the time, with a minimal amount of the one-on-one interaction with caretakers that allows personal bonds to develop. This group of adopted children has been the subject of perhaps the most careful studies ever done of the effects of maternal neglect. The results show conclusively that the effects of such minimal care are more damaging than even ardent advocates of attachment theory had imagined.[50]

The near-universal experience of the adoptive parents has been that these children suffered from an array of physical, emotional, psychological, and cognitive problems resulting from their orphanage experience. One study found that 78 percent of the children it evaluated were delayed in motor skills, social skills, and language skills when they were adopted. While those children who were adopted after the age of six months had more severe difficulties, even the younger babies were more likely than average children to suffer impairments in all of these areas.[51] Ronald Federici, a developmental neuropsychologist who evaluated about one thousand of these adoptees, made the point that "not only lack of nutrition but also of stimulation and of emotional contact, can inhibit the development of brain systems."[52] The numerous cognitive impairments of the adopted children presented a difficult barrier to successfully overcoming their emotional problems, some of which include the inability to form bonds with the adoptive parents, violent outbursts, distrust of family members combined with alarming effusiveness with strangers, and hypersensitivity to physical touch. A recent *New York Times Magazine* feature on adopted Romanian children concluded that "for a very young child, the lack of an emotional connection with a consistent caretaker can be deeply damaging."[53] This amounts to an endorsement of the fundamental premise of attachment theory.

Substitute Parenting

What implications, if any, does this have for the intensifying debate over the adequacy of day care centers and current proposals to expand day care subsidies? Many feminist thinkers—among the earliest advocates of the widespread use of day care by working mothers —originally made the case for day care both as a necessary component of women's professional self-fulfillment *and* as an entirely adequate, if not superior, alternative to full-time maternal care. (This will be explored more fully in the chapter which treats the development of anti-natalist feminism).

Feminist advocates of child care, long dismissive of attachment theory as sentimental propaganda, maintain even today that the reliance of working mothers on professionalized day care for their children presents no drawbacks to the child's normal development, even in infancy. One of the foremost opponents of attachment theory, psychologist Diane Eyer, argues that the maternal influence on children is overstated. "Children are profoundly affected by an array of people who interact with them," she has written, "by the foods they eat, by the music they hear, by the television they watch, by the hope they see in the adult world and by the institutions—especially schools—they attend." Kate Millett makes the case for the *superiority* of day care to maternal care: "The care of the young is infinitely better left to trained professionals rather than to harried amateurs with little time nor taste for the education of young minds."[54] A prominent women's magazine advised women not to fret too much about the quality of day care centers: "What if the child care you find isn't ideal? Well, home life isn't ideal either.... If the place you found has a responsible staff and a safe, stimulating environment, it's probably fine."[55]

So far, the evidence regarding our vast and unprecedented experiment in substitute parenting indicates that breezy reassurances are unwarranted. In fact, it appears that the children of day care exhibit some of the same debilitating emotional, psychological, cognitive, and even physical problems displayed by children adopted from the Romanian orphanages.

In their book *The Day Care Decision*, William and Wendy Dreskin paint a disturbing picture. The Dreskins operated a nonprofit nursery school in the San Francisco area for several years, until increasing demand by dual-earner couples persuaded them to expand their operation to a full-fledged, day-long child care center. The center was staffed with top-quality teachers and the curriculum was excellent, but the Dreskins found that the effects of day-long day care on young children were often traumatic. Preschoolers who seemed to be doing well in the morning-only nursery school began lashing out, withdrawing, and crying for hours on end. Some children even lost abilities they had acquired.

"For two years we watched day care children respond to the stresses of eight to ten hours a day of separation from their parents with tears, anger, withdrawal, or profound sadness," the Dreskins write, "and we found, to our dismay, that nothing in our own affection and caring for these children would erase this sense of loss and abandonment." Despite the fact that when they began the program they "did not have the slightest suspicion that there might be a serious problem with even the best day care," their experience with the children at the center was enough to convince them otherwise. "We were so distressed by our observations that we closed the center."[56]

Other anecdotal evidence abounds. In a recent issue of *The American Enterprise* devoted to the day care debate, editor Karl Zinsmeister assembled much of that evidence in what is perhaps the most comprehensive summary of the issue to date. Even those who make their living in the booming child care industry are not convinced that day care is an adequate substitute for parental care. Zinsmeister relates that he received a flood of personal letters critical of day care in response to an article he wrote on the subject for a prominent national magazine. What surprised him most was the considerable number of the letters from day care workers themselves. Many were deeply disturbed by what they had seen on the job.

One letter from a former day care worker stated that "it was impossible for us even to approach the level of care we believed a child needed. . . . I watched children being traumatized as workers came and went. I observed the disenchantment they suffered, and the hostility they developed. . . . Before my year in day care work was over, my co-workers and I were able to convince five of the 12 mothers whose children we cared for that they would be happier, and that their parent-child relationships would be healthier, if they would quit their jobs and would stay at home with their children." In a *Wall Street Journal* interview the head of an Illinois day care center said, "I'm torn. I want [the kids] to feel safe and secure, but this is not their home. Parents think we can substitute for family, but we can't."[57] Author Penelope Leach quotes a day care worker saying that "when I have children of my own I will use everything I know to look after them myself. I'd die rather than put a child of mine in the place where I work."[58]

The evidence that day care affects children in profoundly detrimental ways is not merely anecdotal. Numerous studies in recent years confirm what anecdotal evidence implies: that paid "day care professionals" cannot substitute for maternal affection. Child psychologists in London found that children in group care showed significantly less "affection and emotion" than children cared for at home, also noting a higher level of aggression among those in group care.[59] It also appears that the negative consequences of significant time in day care last longer than experts once imagined. A RAND Corporation study in 1989 showed "a statistically significant adverse effect" on children's intellectual ability deriving from their mothers' reliance on group-care facilities as a result of their employment.[60] Recent studies in both the United States and Norway found no measurable relationship between IQ and behavior, but noted "higher levels of behavioral problems" among children who had a significant amount of nonparental care in their first four years.[61] "Passive withdrawal" from social activity and environment is much more common in children of mothers not "readily available," according to another study.[62]

The typical day care center is simply not a place where a preschooler is likely to get the constant personal care that he requires. Day care centers in general operate as if the "minimal care" theories popular in the immediate post-World War II period have never been challenged, let alone debunked. Instability and discontinuity of care are a given in a system of professionalized, nonparental care. When applied to a day care setting, normal work routines such as split shifts, lunch breaks, sick leave, vacations, and training courses translate into more people the child has to interact with. Some studies have suggested an average of seven different people a day and fifteen a week for each day care child. One estimate reported that 41 percent of all caregivers quit their positions each year. With the increasing demand for day care, this staff turnover has accelerated dramatically over the past decade. This kind of turnover is particularly traumatic for babies, who have to communicate their needs nonverbally.

Add to this discontinuity of primary caregiver the fact that in most centers, the child-to-staff ratio is inadequate. The government's own National Child Care Survey estimated that in centers caring for one-year-olds, the average group size was ten children, and the average ratio of children to staff seven to one. Since much of the care of a child of this age consists of feeding, diapering, and cleaning, little time remains for an overworked child care professional to interact with the child and provide stimulation beyond the minimal physical essentials. Older children in day care, thought to require less personal attention, are frequently crowded into groups of fifteen.

Regimentation and routine are ever-present aspects of any day care regime, simply as a matter of practical necessity. Unlike the personal attention given to younger children in the home, which can be adjusted to the needs and temperament of the child, the environment of the day care center governs and the child has to conform. Scheduled activities are not so much for intellectual development, as for keeping a large group of youngsters occupied. This is to be expected; day care workers are not, after all, professional educators, but professional caretakers. Their task is more akin to crowd control than to the formation of young minds.

The standardization and routine that are a necessary aspect of the day care environment mean that children must live by a strictly regulated schedule: nap times whether or not they are tired, meal times regardless of when they get hungry (and with no allowance for individual taste), play times with the same preprogrammed activities, often with little variation day after day.

Contrast this industrialized, standardized form of child care with the care a child receives in a home. Defenders of professional day care tend to emphasize the material sufficiency of the day care center for the child's normal development: children will be fed, provided with entertainment, and supervised by an adult—essentially what they would get at home from a full-time mom. But there is more to the rearing of children than these material considerations, and the home as traditionally understood is not merely a physical entity; it is a spiritual environment that teaches behavior, not necessarily through any formal instruction, but through example and tacit understanding. Home includes details that are essential in forming the characters of children: family stories, bits of wisdom, inside jokes; enthusiasms for hobbies, sports, music, or politics; intellectual and literary sensibilities; styles of dress and decoration; tastes in food and drink; ways of celebrating and of mourning; and keeping the peace by means of little tricks that can only be known through intimacy. In short, a home contains the little things that are the lifeblood of human existence.

This does not mean that children will become copies of their parents; on the contrary, children usually are overly conscious of being *different*. But essential to the child's unique personality is that home environment, some of which he consciously reacts against, some of which he unconsciously adopts, all of which influences his make-up. The home is the child's school of personality. It communicates the values by which he interprets the world. The formation of the will and the development of personality depend on the interaction entailed in family life. G. K. Chesterton was speaking of this type of "education"—an education in daily living—when he wrote that young children "require to be taught not so much anything as everything. Babies need not to be taught a trade, but to be introduced to a world. To put the matter shortly, a mother is generally shut up in a house with a human being at the time when he asks all the questions that there are, and some that there aren't."[63] Should a mother feel comfortable surrendering this awesome vocation to some anonymous day care worker whose interest in her child is professional—indeed, financial?

The question becomes even more puzzling when one considers the data documenting the physical health of children in day care institutions compared with their home-raised peers. For very young children in day care, there is an increased incidence of colds and other infections, epidemics of diarrhea and related diseases, more respiratory illnesses, and a significantly higher rate of inner-ear infections that can threaten hearing loss. One study shows that the number of sick days for kids in day care is 30 percent higher than the average.[64]

The health advantages of breast-feeding for infants, which include enhanced protection against many infectious diseases and an array of nutritional advantages, have been well known for some time. Accumulating empirical data also show that, at a later stage of development, breast-fed children are physically stronger than nonbreast-fed kids, experience quicker mental development as preschoolers, and rate significantly higher on IQ tests during their school years. Repeated and frequent suckling, researchers have speculated, stimulates "higher mental processes" in infants and cements emotional bonds (again pointing to the vital importance of a strong mother-infant relationship). Yet despite the near-unanimous recommendation of pe-diatricians and child psychologists, there has been a steady decline in breast-feeding over the past twenty years; currently only about 50 percent of infants are initially breast-fed, and fewer than 20 percent are still breast-fed at six months.[65] A recent study noted the reason for the decline: "Employment outside the home appears to be associated with a substantially shortened duration of breast-feeding."[66]

In sum, the evidence that day care is bad for children (both long- and short-term) is massive and is growing. Yet, with a few notable exceptions, experts have been reluctant to tell parents about the dangers of nonmaternal care—and the advantages of an intimate mother-child relationship—which their own research confirms. Why is this? Several years ago, social science researcher Mohammedreza Hojat published a remarkable article protesting against "the conspiracy of silence [that] prevails among scientists on the importance of motherhood and the family." According to Hojat, "a new cultural mentality of political correctness" prevailing in academia—and enforced by "interest groups, including extreme feminists or those who personally prefer a nontraditional lifestyle"—makes it all but impossible to discuss the adverse effects of nonmaternal child care. He further complains that prominent academics have even suggested "that research on detrimental effects of nonmaternal care must be interrupted or abandoned."[67] Michael Meyerhoff, director of the Center for Parent Education, says that while the vast majority of professionals in the field agree with the proposition that full-time day care is not in the best interests of young children, "because of the strong attacks they'd be likely to get, many people are not saying anything."[68] Penelope Leach is even more blunt, asserting "there is a cover-up going on." That the available evidence unambiguously confirms the irreplaceable nature of the individual care a mother provides, says Leach, is rarely stated publicly for "fear of upsetting the parents who don't provide it."[69] She might have added that it is rarely reported in the media for fear of offending the reigning feminist orthodoxy regarding child care.

MORE OF THE SAME?

In the face of this avalanche of data, the response of day care advocates has been twofold. First, they have called for increased government support for working mothers who use formal day care for their
young children. They want larger tax breaks to make day care centers "more affordable," as well as increased government regulation of
the day care centers to ensure a "higher quality" of care. Second, to
address the increasing "parental-time deficit" facing children, they
have demanded a strengthening of "family leave" laws (along the lines
of those passed in 1993) which would require companies to allow both
more time off for employees after a child's birth and greater flexibility
in work schedules to allow more interaction with the child during the
formative years. Despite the stated intentions, however, both of these
proposals would simply have the effect of reinforcing the very behaviors that threaten the well-being of millions of children.

The notion that subsidies and regulations can cure what ails the
day care industry is, on its face, unreasonable: the higher incidence
of disease, the insufficient individual nurturing of infants, the standardization of environment and activities—all these are "built in to
the system." For example, proponents of "quality" day care insist that
mandating higher pay for day care workers will result in a higher
quality of care and a lower turnover rate among workers. Unfortunately, mandated higher pay would mean fewer workers, raising the
already high ratio of children-to-staff and thus violating another of
the cardinal maxims of "quality" care as described by proponents.
Conversely, proposals to mandate higher adult-to-child ratios ignore
the fact that the whole economic viability of the industry is based on
maintaining economies of scale: the reason parents can afford to
sacrifice a portion of their family income to have someone else take
care of their child is that there *is* a relatively high ratio of children
per caretaker, much higher than it would be at home. The only sure
outcome of more regulation of the day care industry would be to

drive the home-based, informal day care givers (for which most parents have a marked preference) out of business. Significantly, these
"nonmarket" arrangements are the form of care that most parents
prefer when home care is not an option, according to polls.[70]

Making day care "more affordable" by boosting tax deductions for
couples who choose it for their children will encourage parents to
farm out their children to professional institutions and will put pressure on new mothers who have mixed feelings about reentering the
full-time workforce to get back to the career track as soon as possible after baby is born. Forcing companies by law to grant more leave
to their employees so that they can better fulfill family obligations will
send the same message to new parents, the fiction that full-time employment and fulfilling one's obligations as a mother are fully compatible—as long as enough flexibility is granted by one's employer.
Despite the fact that proponents present these as ways of making the
economy and the workplace more "family friendly," both proposals
are quite obviously designed by those whose first priority is to keep
mothers of young children on the career track; the primary concern
is clearly *not* the best interests of children.

The newest initiative of day care advocates shows just how
emboldened they are by the pervading reluctance to acknowledge
unpleasant truths about substitute parenting. Studies which show that
the first three years of a child's life are vitally important to development are now being cited not as an argument for the importance of
mother-care, but as evidence that we need a system of mandatory,
universal preschool care for all children. The reasoning is that professional day care providers are better equipped to meet the child's
developmental needs. In other words, stay-at-home moms may be
harming their children by not putting them in "quality" day care.[71]

The ongoing political debate over day care and family-leave
policy—which can only be expected to intensify in the next few
years—is an indirect acknowledgment of the *real* child care crisis.
More and more children are being reared by someone other than their

parents and outside of the home, deprived of the only environment in which they can expect to receive the personal attention, affection, and energetic devotion they require. While feminists and other day care advocates have repeatedly asserted that government must ensure access to "affordable, high-quality day care" for all who want it, they assuredly are not referring to the only child care we know of that fits that description. What is needed is for someone to make the argument for the best (in fact the only workable) system of child care the world has known: mom.

One may well ask why *that* choice—the choice to devote full time and energies to the raising of one's own children—has become so culturally unacceptable that scientists, politicians, public opinion leaders, and academics all seem determined to ignore the facts. Why is it taboo to suggest that a mother's most noble, even sacred, service to society lies not in professional achievement, but in bringing up her children well, a task that only she can perform adequately, a vocation that entails not only hardship but also unique wonders, joys, and satisfactions? To answer that question, we have to take a closer look at the changes in our thinking about the central institutions of home and motherhood in this country over the past forty years. We will observe a radical change from the popular notions about those institutions that dominated public discussion earlier in the century. And we will see that some of the most ardent and eloquent defenders of the traditional home and motherhood in that period were not "traditionalists," but "progressives."

~ 2 ~

The Vanishing Homestead

A feminist movement that respected the achieve-
ments of women in the past would not disparage
housework, motherhood or unpaid civic and neigh-
borly services. It would not make a paycheck the
only symbol of accomplishment. . . . It would insist
that people need self-respecting honorable callings,
not glamorous careers that carry high salaries but
take them away from their families.

—Christopher Lasch

WHETHER ONE WELCOMES THE CHANGE OR NOT, the way our popular culture regards marriage and family, and more specifically the way
it regards the historically female family role of mother and homemaker has undergone a complete makeover. Since the 1960s the term
"homemaker" has taken on a connotation approximating "deadbeat."
It is true that many women still regard these traditional roles more
favorably than would, say, Betty Friedan, who called the home a "comfortable concentration camp" for women. But simply on the basis of

33

the pronounced trends towards surrogate parenting, institutional care of young children, and the full-time professional employment of married mothers, it is clear that the attractions of home and children are not competing successfully with the allure of the workplace for the affections of married mothers. These mothers are voting with their feet, as the saying goes, and their feet are taking them to the office.

The decreasing amount of time that parents spend with their children and the diminishing interest that many mothers display in taking the primary responsibility for rearing those children are not the only signs that children are a relatively low priority for many families. Perhaps a more fundamental sign of the diminished importance of children in our culture is that married couples are having fewer and fewer of them. The rise in out-of-wedlock births in the United States in the past thirty-five years has been the subject of much recent commentary. Little noted in that renewed discussion, however, is the fact that this astounding increase—from about 7 percent of all births in 1965 to about 32 percent (almost one third) today—owes as much to the decline in the reproductive rate among married women as it does to the increase of births among single women.[1] That is, the proportion of illegitimate births has soared in large part because there are so few babies being born to married couples.

Seen in this same context, the Baby Bust among American women (the fertility rate having declined from approximately 3.5 children per couple in 1960 to around 1.9 in 1998, below the so-called "replacement rate") is a phenomenon restricted to married women. Single women, on the other hand, have been experiencing a veritable baby boom: their fertility rate has doubled since 1975.[2] Recent celebrations of a decline in the rate of teen pregnancy as a positive cultural sign have all but ignored the fact that *illegitimate* births to teens remain at historic highs; it is only the sharp drop in the birth rate of married teens that has resulted in the overall decline in teen pregnancy.[3] Indeed, the decline in pregnancy among married teens is just part of an overall fertility decline among married women, for whom the birth rate has continued to fall in the last decade.[4]

It might appear that the rising fertility rate among unmarried women and the falling fertility rate among married women are responses to economic conditions, positive and negative. Indeed, much of the consensus (inasmuch as one exists) for reforming public assistance programs derives from the reluctant realization on the part of some long-time proponents of welfare that the unintended effect of programs designed to provide assistance to indigent single mothers has been to subsidize illegitimacy. As a result of the benefits that are available to women with dependent children regardless of their marriage status, government has become, for many young impoverished women, a more reliable source of regular income than a husband. An illegitimacy rate of over 70 percent in the black community is, in itself, ample proof that the mother-state-child model of family structure has replaced the mother-father-child norm in fairly substantial sectors of our society.[5]

The case for economic incentives governing fertility rates is more difficult to make with regard to married women, but here too there is compelling evidence that decisions about childbearing are at least influenced by financial considerations. Interestingly, the correlation is the opposite of what one might expect: statistics consistently show that the higher the total family income of a married woman's household, the less likely she is to give birth. Evidently, at least in modern America, economic security does not breed large families.[6]

There are, however, factors more relevant than family income, which has enjoyed a modest rise over the past twenty-five years only because of the massive influx of married women into the workforce (the average wage actually declined over this period).[7] Vastly more important than family income in childbearing decisions for married women is career orientation. Working wives have many fewer children than those without labor force commitments, and *expectations*

of childbirth—an important measure of orientation towards family—
are highest among wives not committed to careers and lowest among
those who are career-oriented.[8] Wives who work also have the highest rates of childlessness. The only group among married women not
contributing to the fertility decline of the past thirty-five years are
those least interested in careers. Women who work have fewer children (about one-half child less per woman on average—a statistically
sizable difference).[9]

Couldn't it be the case that married women have been driven into
the workforce by economic pressure, which in turn has resulted in a
lower birth rate? It is certainly true that in order to keep family income from sliding and to maintain an accustomed standard of living, more and more wives—especially those whose husbands are not
on the "high-earner" end of the income spectrum—feel compelled to
contribute to the family's income. Numerous surveys have shown that
substantial majorities of working mothers would either cut back their
work hours or cease work entirely if they could afford it.[10]

But it is also true, as critics of the "economic necessity" theory
point out, that the trend toward the workplace among married mothers with young children is most pronounced precisely among the
group that can least claim economic necessity: the wives of high-earning husbands.[11] And the influx of wives into the workforce in large
numbers began to occur before the downturn in men's wages which
has marked the period since the early 1970s (the large-scale entry of
married women into the labor market may, in fact, have been a major contributor to that downturn, as we will see). At the very least,
we can conclude that the enormous changes in work patterns among
married mothers cannot be explained solely in economic terms.

Economic factors should never be disregarded, but cultural incentives have their own dynamic that almost irresistably change a
society's mores. A large part of the reason that home and children
have failed for many women to compete with the allure of a professional career is that the value our culture places on the activities of

childrearing and homemaking has never been lower than it is now. The low prestige of stay-at-home motherhood is one aspect of a relentlessly materialistic worldview that rates any activity by its "market value" and scorns any activity that has no immediately apparent and measurable worth. Indeed, the popular concept of marriage itself has gradually changed from a lifelong relationship of mutual dependency and service into a capitalistic model of a temporary arrangement from which both partners derive some tangible benefit. Recent studies have shown that when considering marriage, men look at the earnings potential of a prospective partner and are less concerned with qualities of character that they would desire in the mother of their children.[12] Marriage becomes simply a domestic arrangement of financial convenience between two partners pursuing separate "career tracks," barely distinguishable from other domestic arrangements.

But the invasion of economic terminology and market analysis into the domestic sphere is in itself a testament to the demise of the popular ideal of the homeplace that prevailed from the beginning of the industrial era until quite recently. The home was seen as precisely that part of society exempt from the forces of the marketplace, an oasis of cooperation in a competitive economy, a refuge where the life of the family—which that economy exists to serve—is nourished.

A cultural revolution has taken place, and we are almost too close to it to see it clearly. Whereas a devoted mother and homemaker was once regarded as performing the greatest possible service to society— forming young hearts and minds in a heroic effort requiring selfless devotion of time and energy—the popular conception of the stay-at-home mother (and housewife) today is that of a freeloader who is probably socially and professionally incompetent, and who, in the words of First Lady Hillary Rodham Clinton, "stays home and bakes cookies and has teas."[13] Thirty years ago, when *Cosmopolitan* editor and feminist celebrity Helen Gurley Brown characterized the housewife and mother as "a parasite, a dependent, a scrounger, a sponger

... a bum," her words had a socially divisive and distinctly radical ring.[14] The careerist model promoted by the jet-setting Ms. Brown was then shared only by a small group of committed sister-feminists, while the stay-at-home mothers she attacked were part of the normal and dominant family arrangement. But today such harsh language is scarcely needed, for there is a widespread, if tacit, acceptance of Brown's main charge—that the full-time housewife and mother is an unproductive member of society who only has the luxury (or misery) of staying at home because she has an indulgent (or oppressive) husband, on whom she depends absolutely. The notion of productive and socially useful work being performed by the full-time stay-at-home mom, outside of the market economy, is so foreign to the contemporary mind that Senator Christopher Dodd received hardly any criticism when he praised working mothers in contrast to those who "want to play golf or go to the club and play cards"—that is, stay-at-home mothers—in a recent debate over child care subsidies.[15] The cultural devaluation of the stay-at-home mom is so complete that even a husband who likes the idea of his wife devoting full time to bringing up their kids is frequently unwilling to forgo the extra spending money that derives from a second income.

The female role models held up for veneration and imitation by the popular media are almost exclusively highly educated, independent, career women. Bucking that trend to devote oneself exclusively to home and family today requires extraordinary self-confidence and fortitude on the part of young women who must be prepared to endure both the censure of their culture and the disapproval of their peers. It is no wonder that most college women pursue a course of study that will put them firmly on the full-time career path when they graduate; they are simply following their culture's prescription for success and acceptability. And since no-fault divorce, by undermining all claims of a wife to her husband's income, has eliminated the economic security that marriage provided for women in our society, it is hard to blame young women for hedging their bets by setting out on the career path sooner rather than later.

The standard analysis of the movement of married mothers away from the home and into the workplace holds that it is far from a new phenomenon, but only a continuation of long-term trends that have seen women entering the workforce in greater numbers over the course of the last century. This interpretation is simply not supported by the statistics. As we saw earlier, as recently as 1960 only 18 percent of married mothers with young children were working outside the home; the big change only took place after the late 1960s.[16] Today, well over two-thirds of married mothers with preschool children are in the paid labor force.[17]

The question then becomes: How did such a full-scale flight from of the home take place over a relatively short period of time in a society renowned for an almost religious veneration of motherhood and home, a society that, between 1946 and 1964, experienced a fertility boom among married women as their workplace participation declined substantially?

THE ADVANCEMENT OF WOMEN?

The answer to that question is intimately related to the evolution of feminist ideology over the course of the twentieth century—particularly the way that the women's movement has viewed those central institutions of home and motherhood—and the degree of influence that feminist ideology has achieved at various moments in the popular culture. Since modern feminist ideology began to dominate the institutions that have the most direct influence on popular culture (particularly the media and the academy) in the late 1960s, many assume that the antagonism towards the traditional homemaker and mother which characterizes post-1960s feminism has been part of the ideology of the women's movement in the United States from its very origins. The supposition is that this antagonism towards domestic-ity has been a constant theme among those who have striven to rec-ognize more fully the inherent dignity and rights of women. Feminist historians in "women's studies" departments have made careers out of portraying the history of the women's movement as a steady and inevitable progression toward full professional recognition in the workplace and emancipation from the dreary servility of the home—Friedan's "comfortable concentration camp." In the feminist version of history, the only reason that most women before the late 1960s lived most of their lives as mothers and homemakers was that they were systematically barred from professional achievement by men, who schemed to keep their wives at home to do the housework and child-rearing that husbands wished to avoid.

The true history of the women's movement in the United States and its attitude toward the domestic realm is strikingly at odds with—and more interesting than—this standard feminist picture. From our current perspective, one thing stands out immediately when we study the early advocates of women's rights for their opinions on home, motherhood, and family: their views are much more in keeping with the traditional idea of the domestic sphere as women's special realm than feminist scholars would have us believe. In fact, the impetus for the original involvement of women in public affairs in the United States—and the driving force behind most of their policy initiatives—was to protect women from the necessity of involvement in the labor force and to preserve the special realm of the domestic from the eco-nomic and social pressures that would interfere with the mother's primary task of bringing up her children well.

Our popular notion that women's advancement means their greater involvement in the paid workforce is of very recent vintage. It entirely ignores the fact that for most of our history as a nation, the "advancement of women" was identified with *protecting* them from the necessity of involvement in the paid workforce, precisely with the aim of freeing them to devote their full time and energy to what was traditionally regarded as the superior calling of home and family. Post-1960s American feminism chooses not to advert to the truth that a very large measure of women's political activism in our history has been in the cause of "maternalist" policies, child welfare, and the protection of the domestic sphere from encroaching market forces.

What modern-day American feminists refer to derisively as the "Victorian cult of domesticity" has roots that go back much farther. Tocqueville noted, in 1835, the existence of separate but equal spheres of sexual influence, commenting that American women engaged themselves exclusively in "the quiet circle of domestic employments," noting that "in no country has such constant care been taken as in America to trace two clearly distinct lines of action for the two sexes and to make them keep pace one with the other, but in two pathways that are always different."[18] Catherine Beecher, writing around the same time, saw the mission of the homemaker and mother in explicitly Christian terms. "The distinctive feature of the family is self-sacrificing labor of the stronger and wiser members to raise the weaker and more ignorant to equal advantages. The father undergoes toil and self-denial to provide a home, and then the mother becomes a self-sacrificing laborer to train its inmates."[19]

In the family economy, based on the law of self-sacrifice, the mother was the keystone; in Beecher's words "her grand mission is self-denial." The work of the wife and mother in the family could not be valued too highly; women engaged in homemaking and child rearing were "agents in accomplishing the greatest work that ever was committed to human responsibility."[20] This notion of the work of the homemaker and mother as a noble, indeed holy, calling was all but universal, and was shared even by those who had distinctly "progressive views" on women. At the end of the century famous suffragette Elizabeth Cady Stanton wrote that "motherhood is the most important of all the professions, requiring more knowledge than any other department in human affairs," an echo of Catherine Beecher seventy years before.[21] At the end of the 1800s, the "cult of the domestic" was as firmly adhered to as ever, with women's magazines reaching house-wives and mothers in unprecedented numbers, all uniformly celebrating motherhood and homelife.[22]

Around the turn of the century, socially conscious women began to turn their attention to public policy initiatives, moving away from what was, up to that point, a fairly exclusive involvement with private charities. From the turn of the century through the Second World War, a remarkably widespread consensus existed among women's organizations—regardless of their political orientation—about the approach that public policy should take with regard to women. Almost every one of these organizations believed that attempts on the part of policymakers to improve the lot of the nation's women should be guided by certain definite ideals and principles: 1) a "family wage" (an income sufficient for a man to support wife and children at a certain minimal level of comfort) with the explicit purpose of protecting mothers from having to contribute to the family income out of economic necessity; 2) a "safety net" of government support for mothers who, because of the death or incapacity of their husbands, are unable to provide for their children; 3) legislation protecting women in the workforce from exploitation by setting maximum hours and minimum wages; and 4) greater access for mothers to health education and services, with the aim of lowering the rates of infant and maternal mortality.[23] These principles had the common effect of keeping mothers from having to work outside the home and to support them by every possible means in their primary domestic task of raising their children.

Perhaps the most representative, and the most influential, women's association of the period was the National Congress of Mothers (NCM), which had the largest membership of any women's organization in the country and expressed the dominant cultural view on family issues. The Mothers' Congress is portrayed by feminist scholars— if they mention it at all—as a reactionary traditionalist group, but this is far from the case. Founded in 1897 by Mrs. Alice McLellan Birney, the Mothers' Congress stated that its aim was to carry "mother-love and mother-thought into all that concerns or touches childhood in home, school, church or state; to raise the standards of home life; to develop wiser, better-trained parenthood."[24] The organization's ideology was explicitly maternalist; a mother, in Birney's view, is "divinely appointed to be the caretaker of the child," and it was society's duty to help them fulfill this solemn responsibility. In 1898, at the first meeting in Washington, D.C., Birney elaborated on the maternal theme: "Our appeal [is] to all mankind and to all womankind, regardless of color, creed, or condition, to recognize that in the child lies the hope of the race, and that the republic's greatest work is to save the children."[25] The exaltation of motherhood that the Mothers' Congress represented was not based on soft-headed sentimentalism, but rested on the firm belief that the future of society itself rested on the proper upbringing of children in the home. "Every wrong condition that confronts our nation," said Birney's successor, Hannah Schoff, "can be traced to the home. Infant mortality, juvenile delinquency, increase in divorce . . . have their root in the kind of care and training received in the home and its relation to that received out of it."[26] Eighty years later, more and more sociologists, psychiatrists, and policymakers are beginning to see the wisdom of that common sense assessment.

Despite the public focus on the education of mothers and the enactment of social legislation, Birney had an unabashedly domestic view of the role of women, insisting that all of those on the board of the Mothers' Congress were "emphatically women of the home." In fact, Birney's goal of "professionalizing" motherhood by educating women in all the latest techniques and theory in homemaking and child rearing was directed towards reinforcing the domestic sphere. "It is because most women have not had the knowledge and training which would enable them to evolve the beautiful possibilities of home life that they have in many instances found that sphere narrow and monotonous," as she once put it.[27]

The mission of providing mothers with the knowledge needed to raise their children in a professional and socially responsible manner struck a chord among Birney's contemporaries, and from the very beginning the Mothers' Congress received support from a remarkably broad array of political and social leaders. President Theodore Roosevelt, a Republican, sat on the advisory council; officers in the early years of Mothers' Congress included the wives of the vice president, postmaster general, and three cabinet members; the wife of former president Grover Cleveland, a Democrat, was also an enthusiastic supporter. No one at the time regarded the Mothers' Congress as reactionary; in fact, it was thought rather progressive and enlightened. Over the years, NCM often invoked social justice arguments in support of "protective legislation" for women.[28] It was even endorsed by famous women's rights advocates Susan B. Anthony and Elizabeth Cady Stanton, demonstrating that there was no perceived contradiction at the time between individual political and social rights for women and the maternalist agenda.

None of this should be surprising: an American domestic ideology celebrating motherhood and homelife was predominant at the time, even among well-known progressives. Theodore Roosevelt took an intense interest in the organization and addressed its conventions more than once. In 1908 Roosevelt told the Congress that the "mother is the one supreme asset of national life; she is more important by far than the successful statesman or businessman or artist or scientist . . . .There are certain old truths which will be true as long as this world endures, and which no amount of progress can alter. . . . One of these is the truth that . . . the primary duty of the woman is to be the helpmate, the housewife and mother."[29] Roosevelt was warm in his praise of the traditional mother and homemaker and harsh in his denunciation of those who would depart from the cherished ideal. "(A woman) who deliberately forgoes these blessings . . . why such a creature merits contempt as hearty as any visited upon the soldier who runs away in battle . . . the existence of women of this type forms one of the most unpleasant and unwholesome features of modern life."[30] The soldier analogy was telling: the Christian ideal of self-sacrifice for the greater good of family and country was a constant theme in tributes to motherhood, and from TR—who idealized the military virtues—there could be no higher praise.

On this matter, Roosevelt expressed the dominant sentiment of the nation. The embodiment of TR's ideal, the Mothers' Congress, was probably the most popular women's organization there has ever been in the United States. The membership of the Congress grew rapidly, reaching (under Hannah Schoff) 190,000 in 1920, and over one million a decade later.[31]

Besides educating mothers about their duties in the home, NCM took a leading role in promoting protective legislation, the so-called "mothers' pension" laws being a prominent early example. Rarely has there been such a spontaneous, popular, and successful demonstration of public support for a policy idea in our history; enacted by 40 of the state legislatures before 1920 (most of them between 1911-1913), four more states and the District of Columbia passed mothers' pension bills in the following decade.[32] The mothers' pension legislation authorized direct payments to impoverished mothers to cover the cost of raising their children at home so that they would not have to be placed in foster homes or orphanages. The popularity of the idea of providing aid to poor mothers to allow them to bring up their own children—and the relative ease and speed with which the legislation passed—tells much about the high esteem home and motherhood were accorded. At the time of the passage of most of the mothers' pension bills, no adult males were eligible to receive direct entitlement payments, a situation that did not change until the New Deal.

The notion that impoverished mothers should receive some form of direct assistance began to pick up steam after the 1909 Conference on the Care of Dependent Children, held in Washington, D.C. President Roosevelt, who gave the conference's opening address, himself gave voice to the developing consensus with an appeal calling for the widowed mother to be helped through public or private relief so that she might "keep her own home and keep the child in it."[33] The conference resolution on the need for mothers' pensions reflected perfectly the ideology of the domestic that had held sway since the nation's founding: "Home life is the highest and finest product of civilization. It is the great molding force of mind and character. Children should not be deprived of it except for urgent and compelling reasons. Children of parents of worthy character suffering from temporary misfortune and children of reasonably efficient and deserving mothers who are without the support of the normal breadwinner, should, as a rule, be kept with their parents, such aid being given as may be necessary to maintain suitable homes for the rearing of the children."[34]

The political momentum for passage of mothers' pensions was almost entirely the result of efforts on the part of women's organizations; major labor unions also supported the legislation, for reasons that included both keeping mothers at home and upholding the interests of wage-earner fathers in light of the detrimental effect female competitors for their jobs would have on wages. In 1911, the American Federation of Labor formally endorsed mothers' pensions.[35] The support of women's magazines, which wielded enormous influence, was another key element in the passage. One of the more popular journals, the *Delineator*, made mothers' pensions their signature issue.[36] The National Congress of Mothers' own *Child Welfare Magazine* argued "this recognition of motherhood is not charity. It is justice to childhood, economy to the state, and given for service rendered just as the soldier's service is recognized."[37]

The form the mothers' pension laws took also tells us a lot about the kind of family ideal proponents wished to support. By 1931, close to one hundred thousand families were receiving mothers' aid grants: approximately 80 percent were widows with dependent children; some were wives whose husbands were incapacitated; a very small percentage were abandoned or divorced mothers; and only fifty-five of the recipients in the entire country were unmarried mothers (and those with special "mitigating" circumstances).[38] Clearly, the idea was not that the state is an adequate substitute for the father as a source of family income, but that children in traditional families should continue to be cared for in the home by their mothers even in case of the husband's death or disability. By excluding unmarried mothers and divorced mothers (for the most part) from eligibility, the framers of the mothers' pension laws made it quite clear that their primary concern was to support traditional families when those families suffer financial difficulties from the loss of the husband's income. They were also concerned to take no action that would encourage illegitimacy or divorce. In addition to the criteria excluding certain categories of recipients, there were behavioral criteria as well. Mothers could receive aid only if they were judged "worthy"; examples of unworthy mothers included drunkards, those who neglected their children, and those "living in sin."[39] Only much later, with the welfare legislation of the Great Society were moral criteria abandoned in administering AFDC programs—the direct successor of mothers' pensions. The subsequent explosion of the illegitimacy rate is a persuasive argument that the concerns of mothers' pension proponents were justified.

Concurrent with the almost spontaneous passage of mothers' pension laws across the country was a new perception on the part of women's associations that the needs of mothers and children called for representation in government agencies. These government agencies included the Home Education division of the Bureau of Education (created in 1911 at the prompting of the Mothers' Congress), the Women's Bureau, the Bureau of Home Economics at the Department of Agriculture, and most important, the Children's Bureau, created in 1912 at the height of the movement for mothers' pensions with support from every major private association of women in the country.

In fact, government agencies or departments concerned with the needs of mothers and babies were quite traditional and "maternalist" in outlook and aims, despite being staffed and run primarily by "pro-

gressive" women. The Children's Bureau is a good example. The idea
of a federal department concerned with the well-being of children
originated among the leading women reformers of the "social settle-
ments," those communities dedicated to social reform and the education of women. Florence Kelley of the renowned Henry Street
Settlement of New York and head of the influential National Consumers' League, had proposed as early as 1905 (in a book entitled *Ethical
Gains through Legislation*) a federal bureau to gather facts on child
welfare.[40] The National Child Labor Committee, one of whose leaders was Kelley, continued to push the idea, and in 1912 the Children's
Bureau was signed into law by President Taft. Its mandate was to
investigate and report "upon all matters pertaining to the welfare of
children and child life among all classes of our people."[41] Created with
the full support of women's organizations like the Mothers' Congress,
the new department was to gather data on the state of children's health
and general well-being, to publicize "scientific" information on child
rearing, and to make helpful information available to mothers and
families. The first head of the bureau was Julia Lathrop, another
prominent reformer with a reputation as a progressive. For Lathrop,
however, progressivism included the exaltation of motherhood, which
was, she said, "the most important calling in the world."[42] Her bureau began by focusing on infant mortality and maternal mortality.
The main distinction between the missions of the Children's Bureau
and the Mothers' Congress was the bureau's emphasis on raising the
dignity of motherhood to the "status of a profession"; the bureau's interpretation of "scientific motherhood" included not only educating
mothers about the newest information and technologies, but also
changing cultural attitudes that regarded housework and motherhood
as less important than professional work.

One of the early and most representative activities of the Children's Bureau was the administration of the Sheppard-Towner Act of
1921, which provided "for the Promotion of the Welfare and Hygiene
of Maternity and Infancy." Quite striking in today's rhetorical and

political context is the understanding that Lathrop and her socially progressive colleagues at the Children's Bureau had of "women's health education and services." Today, the phrase "women's health" is a euphemism for the availability of birth control and abortion. But Lathrop understood it to mean provision for the health of mothers and babies. Her description of the Sheppard-Towner Act as a "bill designed to emphasize public responsibility for the protection of life" sounds much like today's pro-life rhetoric.[43]

Like the mothers' pension bills, Sheppard-Towner was supported primarily by women's organizations. *Child Welfare Magazine*, the publication of the National Congress of Mothers, invoked a similarly pro-life theme in support of the bill, arguing that "the country needs every life. It will take several generations to make up for the losses of human life in the war. Never has there been greater need for saving life." The editorial concluded that "Mothers can save 200,000 lives of babies every year if Congress helps them by passing this bill."[44]

Under Lathrop, the Children's Bureau consistently supported the "family wage" concept, using survey data they had compiled on infant mortality to support their argument that the rate of infant deaths was directly linked to insufficient incomes for working fathers, which led mothers in poor families to take on jobs outside the home. "The power to maintain a decent family living standard," according to Lathrop, "is the primary essential of child welfare. This means a living wage and wholesome working life for the man, a good and skillful mother at home to keep the house and comfort all within it. Society can afford no less and can afford no exceptions. This is a universal need." Far from seeing the upturn in women's wage-earning work as a positive sign, Lathrop regarded it as a disturbing indicator of society's insensitivity to the real needs of women and mothers.[45]

Perhaps the most blatant form that "protective legislation" took were the regulations setting minimum wages and maximum hours for women in the workforce. By 1921, forty-one states had passed regulations restricting the hours women could work, and many had also

passed laws prohibiting night work by women. By 1923, fifteen states
and the District of Columbia had enacted minimum-wage laws that
specifically applied to women. Again, the impetus to pass these laws
came from women's organizations, and the main argument they used
in support of restricting hours and setting a minimum wage was that
women as actual or potential mothers deserved special protection
from exploitation by employers.[46]

A secondary argument was that the only way to prevent the evil
of child labor, the industrial exploitation of minors, was by limiting
the working hours of women. Federal inspectors charged with en-
forcing the child-labor laws had found that, without the mother's presence in the home, preventing exploitation of children in the workforce
became impossible because there was no one to supervise children.[47]
Again, women's associations were joined by labor organizations in a
campaign for an eight-hour day for women, largely because unions
understood that the legislation was a way of maintaining a family
wage standard for male heads of families by making women less competitive. But even the Women's Trade Union League joined in the
battle to restrict women's work hours, explicitly using the argument
of "unfair" female competition undercutting men's wage levels to win
the support of male unionists.[48]

Other women's organizations argued for the protective laws on the
basis that marginal women wage workers, like children, were a dependent class of workers who needed explicit protection from being made
to work long hours at low wages. Florence Kelley also supported legislation that would restrict the hours women could work, to keep them
from being exploited. Kelley emphasized the dangers of female wage
"drudgery," and the Consumer's League, in the 1920s and 1930s, filed
briefs in support of protective legislation, arguing that laws to protect women as a class from industrial overwork were necessary because such exploitation was especially damaging for females as actual
or potential mothers.[49] The Children's Bureau also favored this protective legislation for women, and published studies throughout the

period (such as "The Physiological Basis for the Shorter Day for Women") in support of their position. As to the argument that protective legislation had the effect of restricting women to certain traditionally female occupations, the bureau claimed that the natural division of occupations along lines of gender was not affected by laws protecting women wage earners; "modes of production" and "public opinion" were the factors that determined the sexual division of the labor market. "There are well-defined lines," argued the bureau, "between the types of services at which the sexes excel."[50]

Kelley's case for minimum wage laws for women was also based on a desire to protect the "family wage" standard for male wage-earners, but her strategy for achieving that end diverged from the unions' sometimes explicit agenda of making women less competitive in the job market. She saw minimum-wage legislation for women as an initial step towards general minimum-wage laws that would ensure that "unskilled fathers attain a living wage for the maintenance of their families." The courts would be more likely to uphold this new state intervention in the market economy if it were initially restricted to women. In Kelley's view, the effect of a mandated minimum wage would be to perpetuate "the American tradition that men support their families, the wives throughout life and the children at least until the fourteenth birthday."[51] Later feminists would see such an attitude as submission to patriarchal oppression, but Kelley and her contemporaries thought precisely the opposite: financial security for wives, they believed, was necessary for women's empowerment.

The Failure of Equal Rights Feminism

As noted earlier, Kelley was far from unusual in her belief that the family-wage ideal should be the standard of social policy with regard to remuneration of work; virtually every one of her contemporaries, who regarded themselves as progressive social reformers, saw the goal of their efforts as a family wage, supported by law, and the requisite additional benefits to allow married men to support their families and allowing married women, particularly married mothers, to remain at home.

The exception to this rule in the first three decades of the century was a small, relatively insignificant group of "equal rights" feminists, and their failure to endorse the family-wage ideal derived, in the main, from an exclusive focus on the achievement of civic and political rights for women as individuals rather than hostility to motherhood. In fact, the gaining of suffrage was advocated by early feminists as a necessary adjunct to responsible motherhood: "If woman would fulfill her traditional responsibility to children," argued feminist Jane Addams, "then she must bring herself to the use of the ballot."[52]

The new feminists of this period, despite their emphasis on political rights and individual feminine achievement, were forthright in acknowledging the distinctions between the sexes based on the maternal role of women. "The program of feminism is not the mere imitation of masculine gestures and motions," wrote feminist Katherine Anthony in 1915. "[T]here is every need that women should not follow blindly in the path of their brothers but should test the way ahead of them as they go."[53] Where feminists parted company with the mainstream of the women's movement was in their belief that careers (and even servile wage-work) were a liberating development for women which was to be welcomed, rather than an evil—albeit sometimes necessary—which public policy should try to help mothers avert.

Still, they had a high regard for motherhood, like their more traditional colleagues in the women's movement. Crystal Eastman, socialist, pacifist, and journalist, argued that career should be reconciled with motherhood rather than substituted for it. "The modern women," she said, wants more than a "purely domestic career. She wants money of her own. She wants work of her own. She wants some means of self-expression, perhaps, some way of satisfying her personal ambitions. But she wants a husband, home and children, too. How to reconcile these two desires in real life, that is the question."[54] The radical magazine the *Freeman* agreed: "Motherhood can never be the incidental thing that fatherhood is. But on the other hand it is hardly necessary that motherhood and a business or professional career shall be mutually exclusive."[55] While views such as this concerning the "new woman" may have provoked the ire of TR, for whom it indicated a negligent attitude towards the woman's sacred maternal duty in the home, they express undeniable reverence for the role of the mother.

Indeed, until the watershed battle over the original version of the Equal Rights Amendment in the early 1920s brought into high relief fundamental differences over some aspects of protective legislation between feminists and their progressive colleagues in the women's movement, feminists worked closely with other, more popular women's organizations and shared much of the same agenda; first and foremost that of women's political suffrage. The ERA-promoting National Women's Party was perhaps the only national organization representing the radical feminist viewpoint and was far smaller than more mainstream groups like the Mothers' Congress and the National Consumers' League. They often alienated their peers in other women's rights groups with stands like their neutral position in World War I, their support of birth control, and their emphasis on female self-expression in work and personal relations. But before the struggle over the ERA came to a head, Alice Paul's Woman's Party was known simply as a more militant suffragette group, despite its sometimes abrasive style.

Although the logic of their avid support for an amendment to guarantee women equal rights under the Constitution eventually led them to renounce protective labor laws for women as discriminatory, most of the new feminists never abandoned their support of legislation that protected or favored mothers as a specific class of women who performed a valuable service for society. In fact, some insisted on laws that went further than the mothers' pensions in supporting motherhood. ERA supporter and renowned suffragette Harriet Stanton Blatch wrote, after the suffrage battle had been won, that "the most important item in the women's program [is now] the endowment of motherhood."[56] Eastman, too, supported strengthening the laws granting a motherhood endowment. The protective labor laws were another matter. Since all women were not mothers, such special protection was not necessary for those who chose to seek employment outside the home. "The pleas of special protection for women only," read a typical editorial in the Women's Party publication *Equal Rights*, "[take] for granted motherhood as a constant corollary for womanhood."[57] Tellingly, Florence Kelley thought the Women's Party was out of touch with wage-earning women and was scornful of their opposition to the protective labor laws. "Why should an organization composed chiefly of highly paid professional or semi-professional women," she asked, "some of whom have worked themselves out of the wage-earning group, devote itself to defeating the efforts of the wage earners to gain by legislation such leisure as the more favored, self-supporting women already enjoy?"[58] In a sense, the argument was academic; fewer than one-tenth of all married women worked outside the home in 1920.[59]

But while they repudiated wage and hour laws for women as a contradiction of the principle that women should not be treated as a distinct and separate class, most feminists were vigorous in arguing that an Equal Rights Amendment would have no effect on laws that protected or endowed mothers, which they continued to support. The notorious exception was Charlotte Perkins Gilman, who thought that pensions for mothers might encourage a woman to stay in the home, making necessary "her own presence and labor in that family all the time."[60]

Today, Gilman is the figure most frequently cited by feminist academics in their attempt to demonstrate the continuity of modern feminist thought with that of the women's movement in the earlier part of the century. Perhaps this is because she was almost alone among pre1960s American feminists in espousing a version of feminist doctrine that comports with their own views. In her writings and speeches, she displays a consistent and even ferocious hostility to the traditional ideal of the woman as mother and homemaker, and she measures the individual woman's worth solely on the basis of professional achievement outside the home. The turbulent facts of her own life go a long way toward explaining why she was so out of step with her progressive colleagues—the vast majority of whom took traditional family arrangements for granted—and so strangely in tune with the thinking of today's feminists.

Before she became a renowned (if controversial) figure in feminist circles, Gilman had made a failed attempt at the sort of conventional domestic existence that she later attacked with such scorn. But her ambition, her irascible spirit, and her desire for worldly achievement was the source of tension in her marriage from the outset; in a letter to a friend months before her wedding (in 1884), she acknowledged that the prospect of a life as wife and mother was unappealing: "[Marriage] seems to me far different from what it is to most women. Instead of being a goal—a duty, a hope, a long-expected fate, a bewildering delight; it is a concession, a digression, a thing good and necessary perhaps, as matters stand, but still a means, not an end. I look through it, beyond it, over it. It is a happiness no doubt, a duty no doubt; but a happiness to result in new strength for other things; a duty only one of others. It fills my mind much; but plans for teaching and writing, for studying, *living*, and helping, are more prominent and active."[61]

In the event, far from giving her "new strength for other things," marriage and motherhood left Gilman a nervous wreck. After the birth of her daughter, Katherine, in 1885, she suffered severe depression. Unable to cope with motherhood and home life, she summoned her mother to take care of the baby while she recuperated. As Gilman later wrote: "Here was a charming home; a loving and devoted husband; an exquisite baby, healthy intelligent and good; a highly competent mother to run things; a wholly satisfactory servant—and I lay all day on the lounge and cried." She was besieged by recurrent feelings of guilt and inadequacy at being unable to live up to the domestic ideal: "Prominent among the tumbling suggestions of a suffering brain was the thought, 'You did it yourself! You did it yourself! You had health and strength and hope and glorious work before you— and you threw it all away. You were called to serve humanity, and you cannot serve yourself. No good as a wife, no good as a mother, no good at anything. And you did it yourself!'"[62]

Gilman reacted by retreating from home and motherhood, and focused on writing for magazines as therapy. When she told her husband, Walter, of her plans to start lecturing for money on the subject of "human reform," he wrote in his diary: "My darling wife thinks now that she shall some day preach—sermons about health, morality and the like. . . . Ah well, my dearest love, if you have anything to say that will help us, and real solutions to offer for moral problems . . . for God's sake preach! And may you have power beyond all the preachers of all time! Leave me—Leave mother—Leave child—leave all and preach! . . . Go. God help you!"[63]

After a second collapse in 1886, Gilman moved to her mother's house and then to Philadelphia to be treated by a neurologist. The doctor told her she was suffering from hysteria brought on by intellectual excitement, and advised her to "live as domestic a life as possible. Have your child with you all the time. Lie down an hour after each meal. Have but two hours' intellectual life a day. And never touch pen, brush or pencil as long as you live."[64] Instead of following this advice, Gilman separated from her husband and became a full-time feminist writer, lecturer, and reformer. She also became a lesbian, starting the first of a series of affairs that led her to initiate divorce proceedings in short order.[65]

If her private life was highly unorthodox, so was her philosophy of feminism. She not only advocated equality of opportunity in the professions for those women qualified to attain it, but also went far beyond her feminist contemporaries in her expressed disdain for the popular ideal of homemaker and mother. That homemaker was engaged in no productive market activity outside the home made her contemptible in Gilman's eyes: "She is merely working for her own family—in the sex-relation—not the economic relation; as servant to the family instead of servant to the world." This market analysis of the efficiency and usefulness of the domestic sphere and the economy of the home figured heavily in her discussion of the homemaker: "To confine any industry [that is, homemaking] to the level of a universal average is to strangle it in its cradle.... What every man does alone for himself, no man can ever do well—or woman either. That is the first limit of the 'housewife.'" Gilman was obsessed with what she perceived as the inefficiency and incompetence of the domestic sphere: "The preparation of food as a household industry takes up half the working time of half the population of the world. This utterly undeveloped industry, inadequate and exhausting, takes nearly a quarter of a twelve-hour day of the world's working force." The wasteful and inefficient system of the homemaker had persisted for so long, claimed Gilman, only because the mother-housewife role was constantly showered with false praise: "We seek by talking and writing, by poetising and sermonising, and playing on every tender sentiment and devout aspiration, to convince the housewife that there is something particularly exalted and beautiful, as well as useful, in her occupation." Such a romanticization of the homemaker, she claimed, serves to delude the individual housewife that her own efforts are worthwhile: "The permanent error of the housewife lies in that assumption that her love for her family makes her service satisfactory."[66]

Gilman sought to professionalize the tasks of homemaking, emphasizing the cost-saving benefits of collective arrangements: "What we call 'domestic industry' is a relic of presocial time and should be wholly discarded wherever possible.... The legitimate performance of this industry should be by professionals; the preparation of food, for instance, becoming an honored and well paid business and the consumer purchasing it cooked instead of raw; such cleaning as remained in a kitchenless house could be easily done by trained workers coming in by the hour."[67]

Care of children, too, should be left to qualified professionals; leaving the important business of child rearing to amateurs had only led to disastrous results. "In all other human work we have the benefit of the accumulated progressive experience of the ages. Only the culture of babies—most important of all work—is left to that eternal amateur—the mother." Anticipating the child care "experts" of the 1940s and 1950s, she opined that too much contact with the mother was suffocating for children: "Such ceaseless focusing of professional ability upon one child, or a few, is too intense an atmosphere for little ones to unfold in. The mother-and-child relation should be kept wholesomely unstrained ... To share with many other little ones the wise supervision of the teacher for part of the day, and to return fresh and eager to the love of an as fresh and eager mother, is far more healthful."[68] Other feminists often used the popular rhetoric of motherhood in support of their positions, but Gilman's references to mothers exhibit contempt bordering on hysteria: "The record of untrained instinct as a maternal faculty in the human race is to be read on the rows and rows of little gravestones which crowd our cemeteries. . . . Neither the enormous percentage of children lost by death nor the low average health of those who survive, neither physical nor mental progress, give any proof of race advantage from the maternal sacrifice"; "The human mother does less for her young, both absolutely and proportionately, than any kind of mother on earth"; "Human motherhood is more pathological than any other, more morbid, defective, irregular, diseased."[69] Gilman's utopian novel *Herland* envisioned a male-free society in which infants were put in "baby gardens" to be raised and educated by professionals, while genetically inferior women were prevented from breeding, so as to improve the racial stock (Gilman was an early promoter of eugenics as well).[70]

Freed from the burdens of motherhood and housework, women

could then devote themselves to the improvement of humanity, lending their peculiarly feminine talents to the traditionally male world of professional work (and manual labor). Strikingly, Gilman did not believe homemaking or motherhood to be true work, which in her mind was an activity exclusive to the competitive, wage-earning labor force. Work in a trade or profession was "the normal life of every human being ... without which one is a pauper and a parasite"; mothers and housewives were "an enormous class of nonproductive consumers."[71] Women working outside the home would even make superior mothers precisely because "in some trade or profession, [they] are serving both the individual and the collective needs of their children; they help make a better world, and they make better children." For stay-at-home mothers she expressed pure disdain, even to the point of questioning their humanity: "You cannot belong to the human race till you do *human work*."[72]

For Gilman, the home was the enemy of human progress: "For every one of us the main devotion of life should be to Humanity. ... Against the growth of this higher emotion, this social passion, there is no single deterrent influence more sinister, more powerful, than the persistence of this ancient root-form of society, this man-headed, woman-absorbing, child-restricting, self-serving home."[73] Gilman remained convinced of the superior economy and efficiency of collective domestic arrangements even after the failure of a project designed according to her proposals: a twelve-story feminist apartment house in New York City. The cooperative settlement had trained professionals to cook, sew, wash dishes, and do the laundry for each resident family, who had their catered meals served either at home or in a common dining hall. The experiment collapsed in months from bankruptcy and disagreements among the residents.[74]

Just how extreme Gilman's animosity towards home and motherhood was in the context of her time is apparent from her long-running debate with Swedish feminist Ellen Key. In many ways as radical as Gilman, Key worked for married women's legal rights, to legalize free love, and to make birth control more widely available. But Key, unlike Gilman, was still an adamant maternalist. She advocated state payments to mothers, regardless of their marital status, to encourage them to stay at home and care for their children, and thought the movement of mothers into the workplace an unmitigated evil. Her criticisms of Gilman are devastatingly accurate: Gilman's program, wrote Key, "rests on three unproved and undemonstrable assumptions: first, that woman's mental and spiritual work in the home, the creating of a home atmosphere, the management of the housekeeping, and the upbringing of children, is of no 'productive value'; secondly, that parents are incapable of acquiring proficiency as educators unless they are 'born' educators; thirdly, that nature amply provides such 'born' educators, so that the many thousands of institutions—with a professional mother for about every twenty children—could be supplied with them in sufficient quantity and of excellent quality."[75] Key's critique sounds positively prophetic today, when the poor quality and insufficient quantity of child care providers is a common complaint of working mothers.

The really striking thing about Gilman in relation to the rest of the progressive women reformers of her era was how anomalous her views actually were. Her contemporaries, almost without exception, understood that the attainment of full civic and political rights for women as citizens and voters did not require women to be treated in precisely the same way as men, either under the law or in the workplace. "The political rights of citizens are not properly dependent upon sex, but social and domestic relations and industrial activities are," said Florence Kelley. "Women cannot be made men by act of the legislature or by amendment to the Federal Constitution. The inherent differences are permanent. Women will always need many laws different from those needed by men."[76]

After the defeat of the feminist forces in the battle over the Equal Rights Amendment in the early 1920s, Gilman began to be regarded as an antiquated irrelevancy, her ideas no longer granted a hearing even in feminist circles. In 1930 she wrote to a friend "I greatly miss my audience—no lectures wanted any more, and books not taken."[77] Not one of her numerous books remained in print, and when the feminist International Congress of Women made a list of the hundred best books by women authors in the previous century, they completely omitted her work.

An early advocate of euthanasia, Gilman was unwilling to face the physical decline and suffering resulting from inoperable breast cancer, and in 1935 she committed suicide with an overdose of chloroform. Ever ahead of her time, she declared in her suicide note that "public opinion is changing on this subject. The time is approaching, when we shall consider it abhorrent to our civilization to allow a human being to lie in prolonged agony which we should mercifully end in any other creature. . . . Believing this choice to be of social service in promoting wiser views on this question, I have preferred chloroform to cancer."[78]

By the time Gilman took her own life, the new feminist notion that the advancement of women entailed the abandonment of the home as women's special sphere as well as the annihilation of all the special legal, economic, and social structures society had erected to protect the interests of women (in both the home and the workplace) had suffered an apparently mortal blow. In the era of Franklin Roosevelt's New Deal, the women's movement had moved on to more pressing matters, such as how to prevent further erosion of the family wage during a depression, with businesses more and more inclined to cut labor costs (one way was by hiring cheaper women workers).

It is significant that the person to whom FDR turned to handle such matters was also the first woman to hold a cabinet-level position in the U.S. government. As secretary of labor, Frances Perkins worked tirelessly to strengthen protective labor laws for women, to federalize state laws providing pensions to mothers, and in general to make the family wage the standard by which management's fulfillment of its obligations to labor should be measured. The 1930s are often portrayed by today's feminists as a period when the women's movement had stalled because of the country's preoccupation with the depression and because of the misguided maternalism of the popular culture, but it was this decade that saw the gains of the previous twenty years codified in federal law.

Central to both the Social Security Act of 1935 and the Fair Labor Standards Act of 1938 were provisions enacting mothers' pensions on the national level, maternal and child health care, protective labor legislation, and the abolition of child labor. In fact, these New Deal measures received widespread support from the same network of politically active women that had achieved their implementation on the state level. The National Congress of Mothers (by this time the National Congress of Parents and Teachers), cited as an example of reactionary traditionalism by some feminist writers and historians, was a key supporter of the New Deal legislation, including the Social Security Act which nationalized mothers' pensions in the form of (Title IV's) Aid to Dependent Children (ADC).[79] A precursor to the Aid to Families with Dependent Children (AFDC) legislation that was the cornerstone of the Great Society's welfare program in the 1960s, ADC left eligibility requirements for payments to the discretion of the states, and almost every state did not grant payments to unwed mothers.[80] Crafted with the help of Florence Kelley at the Children's Bureau (an agency of the Labor Department), ADC provided assistance only to those whose husbands failed to support them, with the intention of discouraging wage work for mothers (it was only with Great Society "reforms" that eligibility requirements changed, with most of the benefits now going to unmarried and divorced mothers). Thus did the federalization of the protective legislation advocated for so long by women's movement activists continue to reinforce traditional concepts of family structure and morality.

The embarrassing fact is that the radical feminist project of getting married mothers out of the home and into the workplace made relatively little progress before the 1960s. But modern feminist orthodoxy has a standard explanation according to which women's organizations retreated from social activism after the early 1920s, went on the defensive, and abandoned their original mission of carrying feminine ideology into the realm of public policy, de-emphasizing social concerns and retreating back into an exclusive focus on private family life. Many of these organizations lost their maternalist political focus and no longer attempted to bring their feminine perspective to public policy, taking up less progressive concerns.

In truth, since much of their agenda of protective legislation and maternal-infant health had been achieved in the states and then mandated nationally in the New Deal legislation of the 1930s, organized women's groups and influential progressive women in the government turned to achieving a family-wage standard. In this, too, they were largely successful. Following the economic dislocations of the Great Depression and the Second World War, Florence Kelley's hope to institutionalize "the American tradition that men support their families, the wives throughout life and the children at least until the fourteenth birthday" came ever closer to achievement.[81] It has been estimated that by 1960 a family wage was paid by 65 percent of all employers in the United States, and by over 80 percent of the major industrial companies.[82] Although feminist historians today call the family-wage ideal a "myth" designed to keep married women oppressed, few myths have come closer to becoming a reality.

THE ASSAULT ON THE HOMEMAKER

By the postwar baby boom of the 1950s, the policies of the social feminists had largely achieved their goals: American mothers were more economically and culturally secure in their homes than ever before, so secure that fertility among married women was actually going up for the first time in a hundred years; between 1945 and 1965, the fertility rate doubled and divorce declined significantly among college-educated women.[83] But just when the aims of social feminists had

seemingly been secured, the agenda of politically active women's organizations and government agencies involved in advancing the interests of women and children underwent a startling change. The
contrast between the guiding principles of the women who helped to
shape family policy in the first half of the twentieth century and those
of the modern-day feminists who have done so much to shape popular attitudes and public policy since the 1960s could not be more
dramatic. A reaction against the old exaltation of motherhood set
in—in part reflecting the influence of the minimalist child rearing
theories of postwar sociology departments—which has endured to
this day.

A 1957 conference on "Work in the Lives of Married Women" il-
lustrated the turnaround in the thinking of women's organizations
and government agencies with regard to women, work, and family. In
the keynote of the conference, a prominent member of the Children's
Bureau, Katherine Brownell Oettinger, insisted that "we cannot real-
istically expect to reverse" the trend of mothers working in ever larger
numbers (this before the trend really took off), and that policies directed toward keeping mothers from having to work out of economic
necessity should be abandoned. Aside from the argument of inevi-
tability, there was another reason to dispose of the old policy pre-
sumptions: evidence was, supposedly, no longer compelling that the
absence of a mother through work was damaging to the child. "On
the basis of our present information," she stated to the conference, "we
do not believe it is necessarily damaging to a child to be separated
from his mother for substantial periods during the day, if adequate
substitute care is provided." No known study, she claimed, "has established a causal relation between maternal employment and either
juvenile delinquency or the maladjustment of children." Besides, the
higher standard of living enjoyed by the family of a working mother
would provide "richer opportunities for the children and open up
avenues to more satisfactory careers in the future," and the "chronic

guilt, conflict, or deep dissatisfaction" of mothers who wish to work outside the home but do not takes a "toll on children" perhaps as great as that taken by the mother's absence. Oettinger suggested that single mothers be made eligible for ADC grants because they made up "a disproportionate number of mothers who work by force of economic need," contradicting the notion of the social feminists that illegitimacy should never be encouraged. Summing up, Oettinger stated that she did not regard the phenomenon of working mothers with alarm because of her "faith in mothers and faith in the inventiveness of our society." She noted that "all the evidence points to the infinite capacity of the family to change—to change its composition, to redefine the way it shares the care of children with other social institutions—and yet to retain its over-all responsibility for them."[84]

Other conferees were just as sanguine about the malleability of traditional family roles, criticizing the notion that some sort of norm should dictate the desirability of mothers working. Said one: "It is clear that there is no single best way of organizing family life. Some mothers should work while others should not, and the outcome for the children depends upon many factors other than the employment itself." The "conference findings" concluded that the "pattern of work outside the home for wives and mothers has had, by and large, desirable social and economic consequences."[85]

By the late 1960s, such tentative and ambiguous assertions questioning the old policy assumptions about the desirability of mothers in the work force had given way to a frontal attack on the old ideal of protecting the housewife and mother from the necessity of working. In short order, a positive animus toward the heretofore sacrosanct cultural icons of motherhood, home, and family began to pervade the writings of feminists in academia, social science, and journalism, having the effect of desensitizing the popular culture to the devaluation of the status of the housewife and mother. As prominent feminist author Jesse Bernard was later to admit, "it was not until the late

1960s that motherhood became a serious political issue in our country."[86] Before the dawning of the age of the new feminists, motherhood was thought to lie outside the political realm.

The 1966 founding statement of the National Organization of Women would have been regarded as anathema to the old family-wage feminists: "We believe that a true partnership between the sexes demands a different concept of marriage, an equitable sharing of the responsibilities of home and children and of the economic burdens of their support."[87] No longer would there be any attempt to protect mothers from the necessity of wage work; in fact they should be encouraged to share in meeting the family's economic needs. "Every feminist, radical or otherwise," wrote Jane Mansbridge, "knows that when people start talking about the home as women's 'special sphere,' they are constructing a rationale for excluding women from economic and political power."[88] The family-wage feminists of a previous generation, so concerned about protecting that sphere, would have been surprised at this conclusion.

Once it was determined that the goal of the new feminist activists was an equal share of workplace involvement with men, it was clear that the housewife constituted the enemy. After Betty Friedan's *The Feminine Mystique* (enthusiastically received by the popular media) made it culturally acceptable to attack directly the old icon of the American mother at home, the anti-domestic rhetoric of the new feminists reached a higher pitch. Feminist sociologist Jesse Bernard characterized the housewife as a "nobody" who "must be slightly ill mentally."[89] Professor Carolyn Heilbrun called the housewife a "female impersonator" who wasted her time "fulfilling needs of others."[90] The reason for the outright hostility to women who did not choose to work was apparent. As Jane Mansbridge put it, "The very existence of full-time homemakers was incompatible with many goals of the women's movement.... Women can never hold half the economically and politically powerful positions in the country if a greater proportion of women than men withdraw from competition for those positions. More important, if even 10 percent of American women remain full-time homemakers, this will reinforce traditional views of what women ought to do and encourage other women to become full-time homemakers, at least while their children are very young."[91] Feminist author Kate Millett was even more blunt: "The family, as that term is presently understood," she wrote, "must go."[92]

In retrospect, it becomes clear that the true importance of the Equal Rights Amendment—resurrected by the feminists of the 1970s—was its attack on the homemaker. Barbara Ehrenreich agrees, writing "what was at stake in the battle over the ERA was the *legitimacy* of women's claim on men's incomes."[93] The desire to eliminate the mother-homemaker option as a viable alternative for women also explains the enthusiastic support feminists gave to no-fault divorce laws, which undermined any notion of a wife's right to economic support from her husband. Although the revived ERA was narrowly defeated, the new feminists were largely successful in undoing what family-wage feminists had achieved over the previous six decades. The anti-maternal agenda of the new feminists—no-fault divorce, "reproductive freedom," and even the gender integration of the workforce to some extent—was largely achieved through the imposition of policy by judicial decisions and executive orders rather than democratic referendum, as we will see.

But how could the new feminists explain the fact that the very policies they were overturning had been carried through by women activists with an agenda and a view of justice for women diametrically opposed to their own? In order to propagate the notion (central to their ideology of women's *liberation*) that before the dawn of modern feminism mothers stayed at home to raise their children only because they had no alternative, feminist writers have been forced into a tortuous and self-contradictory interpretation of the pre1960s women's movement, its goals and its guiding principles. According to the feminist version of events, it was only with the industrial revolution and the resulting specialization of labor that the "modern" conception of motherhood began to take root; before that, the development and happiness of young children was essentially regarded with indifference and the roles of the parents with regard to child care were basically interchangeable. With the economic value of children greatly diminished in a nonagricultural system, the conception of the home as a separate sphere of love and affection, outside of economic life, began to dominate the popular culture. The status of home and family reached its peak around the turn of the century and since then has undergone a slow, steady erosion as family size has declined. The romantic popular idealization of home and motherhood—designed to keep women happy with their domestic lot—slowly lost its capacity to keep women at home as married women entered the workforce in ever larger numbers.

It was only through the imposition of this revisionist history that new feminists were able to fit the family-wage feminists into their storyline of progressive emancipation from domestic bonds. The actual history of women's political, social, and labor force involvement in the twentieth century is quite difficult to reconcile with this version of events. In reality, until the dramatic cultural changes of the 1960s, it was not only traditionally-minded, but perhaps especially politically progressive women who fought to protect the separate sphere of the domestic and the mother in the home from the harsh necessities of wage work.

For the new feminists, then, the protective legislation becomes important not for its content, but for showing American women becoming conscious of their political power. Mothers' pensions, the Sheppard-Towner Act, and other early protective legislation are important because they show women becoming politically active outside the home, taking a leading part in crafting laws and lobbying for legislation; significant insofar as they demonstrate a growing awareness of female responsibility in the community as well as the home. The claim is that this legislation was important because it represents the first example of a distinctly female perspective being brought to

bear on public policy in a direct way. This convoluted argument conveniently ignores that the ideology reflected in this "female perspective" is the "paternalist" exaltation of motherhood and home. That
the agencies charged with implementing and administering the laws
were largely staffed by women is considered more relevant than the
actual policies they were implementing.

One feminist historian even claims that women of the progressive era simply "used the language of motherhood to carve out a place
for themselves in the public sphere."[94] In this process of achieving
"gender consciousness," a radical and completely unrepresentative
thinker like Charlotte Perkins Gilman can then be given inordinate
importance as one who foresaw the process of political empowerment
leading to economic independence, sexual freedom, and ultimately to
a full-scale challenge of the social order itself.

Meanwhile, the true achievements of the women's movement of
this era are mocked or ignored. The "maternalists" behind the protective legislation, according to today's feminist scholars, shared the
mistaken assumption of their time that women "are united by a capacity for motherhood."[95] Entitlements like the mothers' pensions
were, of course, discriminatory, insofar as they excluded unmarried
mothers from eligibility. Protective legislation had actually been ex-
ploitative, because it had the effect of keeping women out of high-
paying industries. Early wage-earning women are portrayed as trail-
blazing pioneers, who heroically overcame the system set up for their
oppression to bring on the modern era of equality in the workforce.
The reality was a good deal less romantic; in one New Hampshire industrial town, 28 percent of the babies whose mothers returned to
work within four months after childbirth died before their first birthday. There was, in fact, very good reason for legislation protecting
women workers from exploitation, and the effects of those laws, and
the efforts made to provide mothers with better information about
maternal and child health, were dramatic. Between 1915 and 1930,
roughly the years that protective legislation was being passed at the

state level, the proportion of infant deaths fell from ninety-nine to sixty of every one thousand live births among white infants, and from 181 to one hundred among nonwhites.[96]

The contention here is not that protective legislation and the other elements of the social agenda of the women's movement in the first half of twentieth century were the most reasonable or the most effective means of achieving a family-wage policy. It could be argued, for instance, that tax incentives, instead of a centrally administered program of direct payments and employment regulation, would have served the purpose much more effectively. I have recounted their agenda and their justification for that agenda in detail to show that their aim was to protect the traditional domestic arrangement and not, like the later feminists, to destroy it. If a small number of earlier, career-oriented feminists were concerned with allowing women equal access to professional attainment, it was always with the understanding that their choice of career over family was not a norm to be imposed on all, or even a choice that the vast majority of women were inclined to make. A sort of tacit agreement obtained between working women and stay-at-home mothers that neither was the adversary of the other and that each would respect the achievements of the other.

All of that changed with the feminist demonization of the housewife and full-time mother by the post-Friedan women's movement, which revived the radical notions about motherhood, child care, work, marriage, and family that Charlotte Perkins Gilman had propounded half a century before. But whereas Gilman's era still retained the traditional American veneration for the home—and the homemaker-mother—by the time Betty Friedan came on the scene in the early 1960s, that ideal had been so eroded by bogus social science research and media hype that she and her followers were able to effect a revolution in the popular culture's view of home and motherhood.

The story of the cultural devaluation of the housewife and mother in the post-Baby Boom era of "women's liberation," its ideological roots, and its success in transforming public attitudes has been told elsewhere (notably in Carolyn Graglia's *Domestic Tranquility*), and I will not repeat the story in detail here. The swiftness of the revolution in attitudes among educated women is not often sufficiently appreciated. Betty Friedan and her followers found a more receptive audience than did Charlotte Perkins Gilman for their message of liberation from the dependence and servility of domestic existence, in part because wage work became less associated with grinding and repetitive menial labor, and new employment opportunities for women abounded in the postwar era.

Why did the family-wage, maternalist orientation of socially progressive, politically active women give way so quickly to what was in many ways its antithesis? The argument that careerism was the only valid option for self-respecting women wishing to do something worthwhile with their lives (and that the exaltation of home and motherhood characteristic of an earlier age was simply a disguised means of oppression) was only able to have such a widespread impact in the 1960s because the domestic ideal of the postwar generation *was*, to a great degree, shallow and materialistic, as many of its critics have charged. The portrait of the empty, despairing, suburban existence of the housewife painted by Friedan in *The Feminine Mystique* struck a chord with many married women in an affluent culture in which ideals such as "self-fulfillment" and the "achievement of one's personal potential" were valued more highly than the self-sacrifice and service to others that had characterized the earlier, less secularized America of Catherine Beecher. Indeed, a good argument could be made that the seemingly rapid rout of the family-wage cultural consensus was dramatic evidence that the apparently vital domestic realm of the 1950s had long since been emptied of the view that the core of the roles of both mother-homemaker *and* father-breadwinner was self-sacrifice. The transformation of the father-ideal from chief breadwinner to chief consumer was probably already accomplished before the transformation of the mother from homemaker to working mom who can "have it all." Success, in the American Dream model of the postwar popular culture was measured by the ability to procure the "good life," with its requisite material accoutrements, rather than the capacity to adhere to one's principles, even in the face of difficulties and hardship—the virtues of the soldier and the mother. Only a thoroughly consumerist mentality would be so susceptible to the argument that women would only be able to fulfill their potential as persons in the competitive marketplace.

That a dramatic devaluation of the housewife and mother has been achieved in both our popular culture and our public policy—largely by feminists—is difficult to deny. Perhaps less apparent has been the simultaneous devaluation of the home. Part of the older ideal of the home—as we can see from the family wage feminists—entailed the notion of a sacrosanct haven from the sometimes harsh, market-driven realities of the competitive economy, a place where man and woman could exercise a high degree of autonomy within a limited sphere. That freedom was, of course, circumscribed by the needs and demands of other family members—primarily one's children, whose education and moral formation took precedence. But within that sphere of genuine freedom, there was a recognition of the vast possibilities and responsibilities, particularly for the wife and mother: to create a home environment and bring up the children precisely as one wishes—no small power.

Today, with all of our means of "home entertainment," conveniences, and comforts, there is a real sense of diminished possibility in the way we conceive of the home. As Berkeley sociologist Arlie Hochschild noted in her book *Time Bind*, much of the refocusing of energy and attention from the home to the workplace arises from the perception that work is where one can exercise control over one's surroundings and where one can find satisfaction in achievement, while home is associated with intractable problems and conflicts where one's efforts go unappreciated or unrecognized.[97] Add to this the successful effort of the new feminists to associate stay-at-home

mothering with intolerable limits on a woman's individual development and with onerous and unrewarding tasks, and it is not difficult
to understand the remarkably cramped vision of personal freedom
that we find so prevalent in American society today, an understanding of freedom limited to the virtually endless possibilities of self-
indulgence and escapism provided to the individual consumer.

Along with the flight from the home and domestic responsibility, we have also seen a decline in civic responsibility as a direct con-
sequence of the movement away from domesticity. In his book
Women and the Common Life, the late Christopher Lasch pointed out
that neighborhood life and locally based charitable activity were never
so vital as at the height of the domestic idealism of the early twentieth century. Far from living a bored and unfulfilled existence in the
home, women were participating in civic life in unprecedented numbers, voluntary charitable organizations throve, and women's organizations spearheaded successful reform movements throughout the
progressive era. Today, because of the lack of available volunteers,
charitable organizations are run essentially as businesses, "nonprofits"
competing with other "nonprofits" for donor dollars in order to pay
their full-time employees a competitive salary. Community and
neighborhood participation has declined markedly in the past twenty
years: while 22 percent of Americans attended public meetings on
town or school affairs in 1973, only 13 percent did so in 1993.[98]

What are the prospects that the vocation of homemaker and
mother will once again be regarded as a worthy and dignified calling
for women? Not very good, so long as society penalizes—in terms
of both financial and social status—women who make the choice to
give themselves entirely to their family's welfare. Husbands, in fact,
put up very little resistance when the new feminists encouraged wives
to break out of the "comfortable concentration camp" of the home and
get to work. It has long ceased to be a source of embarrassment for
a husband to depend on wife for supplemental income; now an entirely different dynamic is at work. Instead of encountering pressure

from their husbands to stay at home, increasingly women are pushed by their husbands to seek work outside the home to bring in much-needed cash. In a social economy where the dual-income family is the norm, even those couples that like the idea of the mother staying at home do not necessarily like the idea of less income and tighter circumstances. And just as with child care responsibilities, there is no indication that men are doing more housework now than before. On the contrary, it appears that the more the husband relies on his wife for economic support, the less housework he performs.

While it is true that the cultural reinforcement of the choice for home and motherhood has all but disappeared, a large part of that reduction in status is due to a corresponding change in our view of work. If the woman who uses her talents as a housewife and mother is accorded less respect than ever before, then it is also true that work in the competitive job market has acquired a higher status than ever before. Charlotte Perkins Gilman's view that only "productive" professional work engaged in for a competitive wage qualifies as *real* work is now the unquestioned assumption behind the flight from the home.

If housework and mother-work are not regarded as real work, what is? What is it that constitutes real work according to our contemporary culture, and why do we regard it as important and valuable, so much so that we are abandoning the home in droves to participate in it? What do we seek in our work, and are we finding it?

Fleeing the Haven
for the Heartless World

*The more women and men do what they do
in exchange for money and the more their work
in the public realm is valued or honored, the more,
almost by definition, private life is devalued
and its boundaries shrink.*

—Arlie Hochschild

THE UNREMITTING HOSTILITY modern feminism evinces for domestic life has had a profound influence on popular perceptions of home and family. The perennial complaint of feminist leaders in the 1990s seems to be on the mark: the younger generation of women now pursuing degrees in universities and careers in corporations is not fully aware of how deeply their own attitudes and assumptions, particularly about work and family, have been shaped by the ideology of modern feminism. Between 1957 and 1976 the number of college-educated homemakers who said they "enjoyed" housework declined from 67 percent to 38 percent.[1] This certainly reflects the perceived cultural status of such work and shows how thoroughly modern feminist thought—once viewed as radical—has been assimilated. The widespread acceptance—perhaps unconscious—of the distinctly feminist view of the home as a place of onerous duties and unbearable restrictions on one's personal autonomy and self-expression helps to explain why most people in our society (particularly mothers of preschoolers) are spending more time in the workplace.

The total percentage of the population over sixteen years of age in the workforce is now at an all-time high of 65 percent, having climbed steadily since 1975, according to the Bureau of Labor Statistics.[2] Not only more of the population are working, they are also working longer hours. Almost every measurement indicates that average work hours for employed U.S. workers—both men and women —have been on the rise since the late 1970s or early 1980s, a trend unique among post-industrialized countries. The increase is most marked among women, but men's work hours are up as well.[3] In the decade of the 1980s alone, time taken for vacations by employees was down 14 percent.[4] Optimistic predictions that computers would mean more working at home and telecommuting have not proved accurate.[5]

Although the trend toward longer hours at work is perhaps most evident in specific professions noted for their competitiveness or "workoholic" atmosphere (such as law and finance), it cuts across the professions and includes both blue-collar and white-collar workers.[6] One recent survey showed that among two important groups of workers—professionals not paid by the hour and individuals with incomes of over fifty thousand dollars—the average is now over fifty hours a week; among small businesspeople, it is close to sixty.[7]

Especially when the increase in the ratio of part-time to full-time workers is factored in, it becomes apparent that the nine-to-five workday is fast becoming a thing of past. Interestingly, objections to this trend have come principally from feminists. Former *New York Times* columnist Anna Quindlen noted in 1990 that "the 5 o'clock Dad has become an endangered species. A corporate culture that believes presence is productivity, in which people of ambition are afraid to be seen leaving the office, has lengthened his workday and shortened his home life. . . . For the man who is paid by the hour, that means never saying no to overtime. For the man whose loyalty to the organization is measured in time at his desk, it means goodbye to 9 to 5."[8] Feminists, of course, have a not-so-ulterior motive in calling attention to the trend toward more time at work solely as it relates to *men*; in the feminist utopia of working mothers and shared child-rearing and homemaking responsibilities, longer average work hours for dad is a big problem. Quindlen fails to mention that one of the primary reasons for the demise of the "5 o'clock Dad" is the disappearance of the full-time mom. If the demands of the workplace have begun to take precedence over the demands of home, it is often because there is no one at home to make demands. The "home" becomes a boarding house where the occupants leave for jobs or day care centers in the morning and check in for food and sleep at night. It could just be that the "5 o'clock Dad" of yore used to have a home to which he looked forward to returning.

As noted earlier, surveys have consistently shown that a high percentage of both men and women cite lack of time for family as a major concern (and a majority respond that they would work less if they could), but there are numerous signs that this professed desire to spend more time at home is only skin deep. Arlie Hochschild notes that workers are not even taking advantage of existing corporate policies offering shorter hours. One 1990 study of nearly two hundred Fortune 500 companies showed that a negligible number of workers take advantage of hour-reducing options (such as part-time, job-sharing, flextime, and work-at-home). Studies carried out in states which have had enough experience with family and medical leave policies so that the results can be analyzed indicate that the leave has been used by less than 5 percent of eligible employees.[9] Although the number of part-time jobs has increased substantially over the past decade, many of those jobs are what used to be called "moonlighting." Those positions are not, it seems, being filled by parents wishing to spend more time with their children: of all working parents with children under twelve, 96 percent of fathers and 86 percent of mothers are working forty or more hours a week. And once at work, employees feel more compelled to stay there: 60 percent of employees went out to lunch from workplace as recently as 1985; only 38 percent did so in 1993.[10]

Employees complain of too little time for their families, yet "family friendly" policies go unused. Why? It is possible these policies serve primarily a psychological purpose and that the mere existence of such options has the effect of making working mothers more secure in their decision to work. In fact, a 1987 study showed that female employees of companies with family friendly policies continued to work later into their pregnancies and returned to work sooner after giving birth than did women at companies without such policies.[11]

Assuming, then, there is some element of choice behind the trend, what accounts for the fact that workers—men and women, married and single—are spending longer hours at the office? Are the objective demands of the workplace becoming heavier, with increasing workloads and pressure on employees to be ever more productive? If so, heightened employer demands and longer average hours have not resulted in greatly increased productivity, which has been relatively stagnant since the early 1970s, despite massive corporate investment in computers intended precisely to boost productivity.[12]

An argument could be made that, as longer hours become the norm in one profession after another, the incentive to use time productively declines. When the workday has clearly defined limits—whether those limits are due to family obligations or are entirely self-imposed—a sense of urgency is lent to accomplishing one's work, and time is used to the best possible advantage in the interest of getting the job done promptly and efficiently. A deadline, like an appointment with the hangman, concentrates the mind wonderfully. When the regular family meal is at 6:30, for example, it becomes a more pressing matter to finish the day's work in time to get home for dinner. If, on the other hand, there are no external constraints on the amount of time one spends at work and employees are rewarded for staying late rather than for working hard in the limited time they are there, office hours tend to become vague and indefinite, and work expands to fill—and kill—the time. Without a definite stopping time for the day's work (or a usual stopping time), the need to avoid distractions on the job, such as personal phone conversations and socializing with colleagues, tends to become less pressing and the intensity of focus on the task at hand diminishes. When employers increasingly equate physical presence on the job with a high degree of company loyalty, a professional attitude, and the capacity to work hard, the effect is often to encourage employees to draw out their work, or to spend long periods of time on nonessential tasks for fear of being seen as having nothing pressing to do.

The pressure to spend more time at work is in some cases, of course, more driven by the objective demands of the job than the preceding sketch might imply. But much of what goes by the name of "workoholism" in the corporate culture of America today could be better described as poor use of time by those whose sense of home obligations—and the time those obligations require—is radically different from that of previous generations. A major aspect of the decision to spend more time in the workplace is the impression that the need for one's services is more urgent at work than it is at home. In countless ways, the mother of a young child today receives the message that her presence in the home with that child is far from vital: the high percentage of her peers pursuing professional ambitions; the wide availability of day care and other arrangements for care of her children; that young women who make the difficult decision to stay at home are held in disdain by the primary institutions that shape cultural opinions and attitudes (the news and entertainment media); and, perhaps most important, that virtually all of the cultural icons held up by the media for veneration are women of professional achievement. This is not accidental: by definition, women outside the public sphere of politics, power, and professional achievement are less visible than women within it, and often those who create the icons have themselves decided to pursue career over family.

While the desire to "spend more time with the kids" that so many American workers express may be genuinely felt, it can prove to be theoretical and abstract compared to the concrete and immediate demands of the workplace. The working mother may *wish* she had more time to spend with the child who spends most of its waking hours in day care, but she *knows* that her boss expects her to be on the job. The dream is more time for family; the reality is more time at work. Meeting the more palpable demands of the job, even if this is primarily a matter of keeping up appearances, becomes a higher priority than meeting the child's demands for more attention, especially when the child is not able to put those demands into words. This is especially the case if one is repeatedly told that "quality time" with a child is more important than "quantity time."

The idea that a little quality time makes up for large amounts of unstructured time spent with one's children signals a radical change in the way that demands on time are perceived by the average parent working outside the home. Hochschild describes how we are taking an ever more leisurely approach to how we spend our time at the workplace, while we emphasize efficiency and time-saving measures at home. As the family schedule becomes tighter, working parents attempt to squeeze closely organized and scheduled activities with their children into the diminishing hours after work, even while time at the office that is spent on activities extraneous to one's job continues to expand. "Personal growth" courses, mandated classes on "interpersonal relations," dress down days, holiday parties, birthday gifts, frequent collective recognition of professional or personal achievements, even on-the-job psychotherapy—all reveal that work has, to a great extent, replaced the home as the place where social integration and personal identity are sought in American society.[13] Both men and women have begun to regard the workplace as a home away from home or, perhaps more accurately, a substitute home. Just as day care centers are becoming surrogate homes for children, increasing demands are put on employers when households and communities fail to exercise their normal functions: health-coverage, sports facilities, stress-counseling, eating facilities, day care, pregnancy leave, and so on. Meanwhile, communities and homes are falling apart from disuse. And the homes of working parents, in the words of Edwin Markham, become "joyless shanties for bolting down food and snatching a little sleep."

The Satisfactions of Work and Family

How is it that, in practice, the office has become a more vital aspect of their existence, as well as a more attractive place to spend a majority of their time, than the home? Without discounting the factor of economic pressure on individuals and families to earn more in order to keep pace with their mounting expenses, it seems clear that many choose to spend time at work rather than home simply because they find more satisfaction and fulfillment at the office. As Hochschild points out, the modern workplace offers emotional satisfactions that seem to be in short supply at home in these days of family strain. "In this new model of family and work life," she writes, "a tired parent flees a world of unresolved quarrels and unwashed laundry for the reliable orderliness, harmony, and managed cheer of work."

Work in the modern corporate office gives one the attractive opportunity to end one's day with a sense of accomplishment, with a feeling of having been in control of events, with the sensation of living and operating in an ordered, structured world. It is, in fact, one of the few places remaining in our society where one can still find the forms of authority respected, the protocol of hierarchy observed, and orders carried out with at least the appearance of obedience, if only because paychecks depend on it. All of this can be very appealing to a harried parent struggling to maintain control, authority, and respect at home. Despite the hypocrisy, gossip, and duplicity of what is sometimes termed "office politics," relationships in the workplace are clearly defined, and the consequences of refusal to operate within the accepted bounds of behavior or to abide by company rules are clearly understood. In the workplace, contracts, relationships, and even employment can be terminated. Increasingly, this is not just a theoretical point. In the U.S. workforce, one person in ten now changes his job each year.

In the modern corporate office, great attention is given to issues such as worker morale, motivation, and environment; every attempt is made by employers to create an atmosphere in which employees feel valued, listened to, respected, and "affirmed" in their worth to the company. Work is regularly evaluated, feedback given regarding one's "performance level," accomplishments are acknowledged and some-times rewarded with bonuses, and suggestions or complaints are duly heard. Individual accomplishment is emphasized: projects are conceived, planned, and carried out; goals are set and fulfilled; deadlines are met; and customers are satisfied. While much emphasis is put on quantifiable measurements of personal performance, a sense of autonomy in carrying out one's work and meeting company goals is also fostered by managers. At the same time, an atmosphere of teamwork is also sought, of worker cooperating with co-worker on the same project or task in pursuit of a common goal. Whole levels of management in large corporations exist in order to maintain an atmosphere conducive to a satisfied, motivated workforce, and increasingly the model explicitly invoked in that effort is the family. Phrases like "building community," "reaffirming bonds of friendship," "trust," "team-building," and "courtesy" are now an important part of corporate culture; the emphasis is on emotional satisfaction, fulfillment of personality, and attainment of a sense of self-worth in the workplace.

The typical corporation motivates its employees by fostering a sense of individual accomplishment, personal autonomy, and control over one's environment. By so doing, it may satisfy the human desire to engage in some creative activity bearing the stamp of individual personality more fully than did most work in the precomputer age of industry. To the extent that these developments have meant a reduction in the repetitive, monotonous, and generally dehumanizing aspects of work in an industrial economy, they are certainly positive and to be welcomed.

But the satisfactions of the modern workplace are somewhat artificial, impermanent, and even illusory, insofar as they are sought as a substitute for the satisfactions entailed in family life. Because the officeplace is, for the vast majority of workers, physically distinct from the home, it tends to take on the aspect of a separate world, becoming an alternative human community to the family, with its own dynamics and its own priorities. At the workplace, removed from the distractions of family life, the immediate goal or project at hand can take on a seemingly transcendent importance, completely out of proportion to its true significance in relation to the things that matter most in workers' lives. That psychological dynamic of work is, in itself, neutral—anyone who devotes their full attention and energies to accomplishing a task will quickly find themselves immersed in the matter at hand, to the exclusion of all else. The question is, what is animating that effort to work hard and well?

The question does not admit of a simple answer. Most people work from a complex set of motives that they themselves would be hard pressed to explain. But traditionally, as has been documented by numerous cultural historians, one of the primary motivations for work outside the home—and the material end toward which that work is directed—has been the sense that one is making possible a home-centered family life.[14] As domestic arrangements have changed radically, and as family time continues to diminish, that understanding of work is losing currency. It is being replaced by a work ethic which has as its end and purpose the emotional satisfaction derived from work, a purpose easily conceived and—in the short term at least—

easily attained.[15] In the long term, however, such an ethic often proves ultimately insufficient as a reason for work. Without a larger purpose and motivation than the mere sense of personal satisfaction and gratification one derives from working, disillusionment—commonly called "burnout"—is inevitable. One recent study showed that almost half the workforce feels burned out on the job. *Business Week* recently declared stress an "epidemic in U.S. business." On-the-job stress has been consistently related to the number of hours a person works each week, which in turn is closely correlated with the level of dissatisfaction with life in general.[16] It seems that as more Americans seek emotional satisfaction from work, more are finding frustration.

In contrast, the satisfactions entailed in the work of a parent, especially that of a full-time mother, are of an entirely different kind. The work of raising children well requires constant hidden sacrifice, unacknowledged and unrewarded by society, often unacknowledged by one's own family—particularly the children themselves. A mother receives little "feedback" from her preschooler about the quality of the job she is doing, and the little she receives is probably in the form of screams for more attention. The satisfactions of motherhood have little to do with ego-gratification or the pleasure derived from seeing the immediate results of one's toil; they are, rather, the satisfactions of complete self-giving to a totally dependent creature. A society that measures success exclusively in terms of material or professional attainment is unlikely to accord much status to the hidden work of the mother in the home. More likely to value the mother's unique contributions is a culture whose ideal is self-giving, be it the sometimes monotonous, consistent toil of the breadwinner borne for the sake of the family or the same toil borne at home for the same reason. It is not mere coincidence that a society in which the predominant view of work was Catherine Beecher's "self-sacrificing labor of the stronger and wiser members [of the family] to raise the weaker and more ignorant to equal advantages" venerated the mother at home, while a society that views work as a means of self-aggrandizement holds her in contempt.

A good mother must have total devotion to her work, but not because of the prospect of payback in the form of immediate results or pecuniary reward. The accomplishments of a day's work of mothering are impossible to quantify and will only manifest themselves, possibly, in the distant future. The truth that civilization itself depends on such intangibles only underscores the fact that the goals involved in the work of parenting are much more remote and less susceptible to analysis based on results than are the market-oriented goals of professional or wage work. The product of a mother's work is not a project or a paper, but a person, with his or her own personality, temperament, and free will. Good parenting requires a type of patience and long-suffering perseverance that can be especially difficult for someone who has become accustomed to the quick, tangible ways of measuring success afforded by the marketplace. When one's task is the formation of character and intellect, success only becomes apparent years down the line, if then. Opposing influences (such as mass media and a child's peers) can, and often do, work against parental influence, and parents can often have the feeling of "going it alone" or, worse, that all their work has been in vain. With the unprecedented power of the media and popular culture, parents may be more tempted than ever to despair of the possibility of control over the product of their work—their children.

But even today, the autonomy exercised by a homemaker and mother is so great that it can be daunting. One has so much freedom and responsibility in bringing up a helpless, dependent baby, and the consequences of the work are so lasting, that the freedom and responsibility involved in marketplace work can seem much less significant and less frightening—and hence more attractive by comparison. Unlike marketplace activity—where there is usually an element of sports-like competition involved—family life is "playing for keeps."

Having the primary responsibility for forming the character and intelligence of another human being is business of the most serious sort. The relationships in family life have a permanence not found in the world of business. And as social science research confirms, mothers and fathers cannot quit being parents, change families, or terminate a difficult relationship with a child without the gravest permanent consequences.

Despite the almost complete autonomy parents have to raise their children, their sense of control over the environment in which they carry out the job of parenting is more limited, in many ways, by outside circumstances than is the control they exercise in work outside the home. The situations a parent encounters in the course of bringing up a child can never really be planned or carefully orchestrated: babies do not follow company rules that are implicitly understood; they have to be taught family rules—from scratch. When a child reaches a stage of rebelliousness, the authority to set or enforce those rules is often challenged. When family rules are broken, remedial action can be taken, but ultimately children are free to determine their own destinies. A boss has the recourse of terminating an employee whose behavior is incorrigible; a parent cannot fire an incorrigible child.

In short, while the satisfactions of family life are certainly not lacking in comparison with those of professional work, they are conceived quite differently. Happiness in family life has less to do with the gratification of seeing one's will implemented or with the tangible results of one's efforts than it does with unconditional commitment—a commitment which will persevere through setbacks, trials, conflicts, and misunderstandings. Part of the attraction of the modern workplace is precisely that the ultimate commitment and loyalty involved is no longer so much to employer, but to career: the ideal striven for is one's own advancement, increased earnings potential, and greater prestige. In a fluid workforce, commitment to an employer becomes more and more contingent on how commitment advances one's career prospects. Such professional advancement is very often sought for the welfare and economic security of one's family—to put a child through school, for instance. But the flight from commitment at home (as shown by the most fundamental measurement: time spent there), and the evidence of the effect of that flight on children, give us ample reason to wonder whether there is not a large element of self-deception involved in decisions made to advance careers, to earn more money, or to increase work commitments with "the good of the family" as their justification.

WHY WORK?

Seen in the context of the elusive search for emotional satisfaction and a sense of personal autonomy, the American exodus from home to workplace accords with our culture's wish for immediate gratification and its fear of long-term commitment—even though many may associate longer hours at work with a spirit of self-denial and sacrifice. No doubt, the "results-oriented" understanding of the purpose, satisfactions, and benefits of work is also consistent with the "bottom-line" business ethic that rules the corporate world. But despite its seemingly evident practical advantages (that is, more income), the question remains: Is this view of work escapist?

The epidemics of burnout and depression in the workplace seem to argue that it is. When not directed toward providing security and stability for family life, particularly the rearing of children in the home, work outside the home loses much of its traditional meaning. While human work certainly has an inherent value (both to the individual and to society) that goes beyond its function of providing the means of sustenance for families, the latter function has constituted the primary psychological basis of most labor down through the centuries. Family life has been substantial enough to balance life in the workplace, not only because it gave the worker the opportunity for relaxation and repose after labor, but because it infused that labor with a deep, even transcendent, meaning. One can work hard and well from motivations other than family, but unless work is animated by loyalties and duties that extend beyond the workplace, its potential to fulfill is greatly diminished. The short-term satisfaction found in work can easily turn into long-term frustration with mundane aspects of any job, or with the insincerity of workplace relationships based on subordination, power, and competition. Unless a higher commitment than mere personal advancement animates efforts at work, the inevitable sacrifices, setbacks, and frustrations can come to seem pointless. A reflection of this is the increasingly common phenomenon of women in their late thirties and early forties who have been on the professional track since high school and have found that promises of "self-fulfillment" through careerism are not all they are cracked up to be. Unfortunately, the decision to start a family is not so easy for a woman to make after she has been pursuing a career for ten or fifteen years.

These misplaced hopes of personal fulfillment associated with the careerist mentality originate in the way that our culture conceives, or misconceives, of work. Today work is primarily regarded as a place of self-fulfillment, a conception of labor that has scant historical precedent. The focus today is primarily on the benefits of work for those engaging in it: emotional satisfaction, a sense of accomplishment or self-worth, power, money, a feeling of personal autonomy—none of which involves service to others. While those benefits have always been an important component of work, the extent to which they now dominate popular literature on work is striking. Other, more selfless values inherent in human labor, values prominent in the traditional Protestant work ethic—sacrifice for the future, service to others, duty to society—fade away as the larger context of work, the motivating principle of that ethic—home and family life—continues to dissolve.

Until relatively recently, the larger view of work as something essentially oriented towards the good of the family was all but universal, and our loss of that vision has been astonishingly rapid. Work weeks of fifty hours or more are no longer cause for comment in many professions, yet even the fabled Organization Man of the conformist 1950s would have thought it strange for a husband and father to sacrifice so much of his time with the family. In a thoughtful column in the *New York Times Magazine*, feminist writer Susan Jacoby rejected the "post-feminist stereotype" of the "Dour Old Dad" of the 1940s and 1950s, who was supposedly "a remote, frequently authoritarian figure with his face in the newspaper and his sensitivities in the deep freeze." She compared Dour Old Dad with the "sensitive" post-feminist Dad:

> Most of our fathers made it clear that their occupations were important primarily as a means of providing for their families. They took pride in their work, but the term they used to describe what they did is significant—a straightforward "job" rather than an inflated "career."
>
> Neither business travel nor 12-hour workdays were as common among the white-collar classes 30 or 40 years ago as they are today. Yet many feminists (of both sexes) maintain that today's men are somehow more "involved" parents than their own fathers—in spite of the absence of "quantity time."
>
> I don't buy it. . . . Whatever their styles as parents, these men stuck close to home. Quantity time. Quality time.

Jacoby went on to speculate that the unfair stereotype of her father's generation may derive from the psychological need of today's parents to justify their own lack of attention to their children: "The current desire to cast our all-too-fallible fathers in the role of awe-inspiring paterfamilias may well be rooted in a need to bolster our very different domestic choices by recasting the past in a more negative light."[17]

The self-directed notion of work as "career" (as opposed to the family-oriented understanding of work as "job") is a conception that could only arise in the post-industrial age, and in some ways it is surprising how long it took to arise. There has always been an implicit tension between the prevailing ethic of work in the United States and the ethic of home, between the old Protestant work ethic and the old ideal of domestic life that prevailed until the 1960s. Side by side with the cult of domesticity went the cult of work, and the very notion of "separate spheres" of sexual influence, with the husband as breadwinner and the wife as homemaker, pointed to the fact that, in one sense, each ideal stood in opposition to the other. The Protestant work ethic (a potent source of America's historical identity and deeply ingrained in the popular consciousness) has always contained a large element of activism in its understanding of work as a virtuous undertaking: diligence, ceaseless activity, and tireless application are all identified with moral rectitude, while evil is synonymous with laziness, passivity, and idleness. Adriano Tilgher had the American model in mind when he wrote that for the modern laborer "it is through work that he embodies in himself the sacred principle of activity, another name for liberty." It is a view of activity that is at once both nihilist and materialist: nihilist in that it instantiates Nietzche's remark that people never feel more alive than when they are busy; materialist in that vigorous work becomes the summing up of all duties and virtues, and since it is by definition productive and profitable, it is exclusively a *marketplace* activity.

The American democratic capitalist version of this work ethic equates financial, social, and even moral status with the degree of individual effort or application of the worker. In laissez-faire ideology, the successful, the hard-working, and the responsible rise to the top; it is only the stupid, the lazy, and the irresponsible who have nothing to show for their efforts. In a competitive economy, one has to enter the game to have the opportunity of winning the prize, and the way one enters the game is to enter the paid workforce. There is a corresponding devaluation, in this ideal of work, of uncompensated labor, of labor engaged in outside of the competitive economy, of "unproductive" labor that produces nothing of market value and hence obtains no profit. In the old work ethic, the home was equated with rest, leisure, and family life. But in associating work exclusively with

market activity, and in maintaining that the market by its very nature puts an appropriate value on all worthwhile human activity, the
traditional American veneration of home life contained a contra-
diciton. However much the cult of domesticity valued—even exalted—home, children, and family, the activities in the domestic
sphere were never considered work.

But family life, of course, requires a great deal of work, and feminist critics are right to point out that free market economic and business theorists have never really put an appropriate value on that part
of the economy that not only produces the workers, but also equips
them with emotional and physical stability, ethics, love, and a sense
of responsibility. Because it is uncompensated, the work of the
mother and homemaker is too often taken for granted in economic
theory, and a materialistic analysis that sees man in purely economic
terms is bound to undervalue domestic work. But the feminist solution—encouraging women to leave the domestic realm for the marketplace where their work (so they promise) will be valued—has only
accelerated the cultural devaluation of work in the home. It has also
succeeded, in many homes, in making domestic work just one more
commodity for which the market has a price tag (and not a very high
one). "In the long term," wrote Ernest Mandel in *Late Capitalism*, the
market "tends to disintegrate [the traditional] family by transforming duties performed by women in the household into capitalistically
produced commodities."[18]

But while this unreasonably strict dichotomy between work and
home, or the sphere of the workplace and the sphere of home life, has
a long history in the United States, there was always a deeply felt necessity to balance intense industry with domestic tranquility. Home
life and the leisure made possible by labor even became, in some
sense, the justification of work in a competitive economy dedicated
to the bottom-line values of efficiency and profit. If the breadwinner
had to package himself so as to sell his labor as a commodity in the
marketplace, at least he could relax and be himself at home. In the

domestic realm, his worth was not judged by the wage his labor could compel.

One of the original exponents of the distinctively American work ethic (and the man often cited as its personification) was Benjamin Franklin. Yet it is revealing to note that with all the emphasis he puts on industry and application in one's profession, his work habits were unacceptably relaxed by today's workplace standards: Franklin took two hours for lunch each day and quit promptly at 6:00 p.m.[19] In practice, the near-universal belief that the fulfillment of private domestic responsibilities and commitments took precedence over—indeed, were the very reason for engaging in—the public activities of professional work and civic life acted as a brake on any tendency on the part of males to take their marketplace involvement too seriously. A popular pamphlet of the mid-nineteenth century entitled *Advice to Young Men on their Duties and Conduct in Life* was typical of the prevailing view: "Those who have least regard for home—who have indeed, no home, no domestic circle—are the worst citizens."[20] When the husband and father has strong ties and obligations that bind him to the home, there is an objective purpose and meaning to his professional work, and he is more likely to work for financial stability than for self-fulfillment and identity.

The Descent into Consumerism

Though our economy has long been one approving of both competition and high levels of consumption, any tendency to consider work as merely the means of acquiring wealth, possessions, and power, was historically balanced by a strong moral tradition, at the center of which was an almost religious veneration for ideals of home and family. When President Theodore Roosevelt said that the mother was "more important by far than the successful statesman or businessman or artist or scientist," he was not simply engaging in empty maternalist rhetoric: he expressed the deeply felt sentiments of millions of his fellow countrymen. In the work ethic that dominated the earlier part of the twentieth century, the monotony and dreariness of much of the work available in the industrial era was taken as a necessary sacrifice for the family. Forgotten or ignored in the modern feminist attack on the notion of "separate spheres" popularized in the United States by Catherine Beecher, is that both women and men conceived of the home as the superior sphere. In their view, the home was the "haven in a heartless world," as Christopher Lasch put it, providing a necessary human environment of love, nurturing, and rejuvenation for the breadwinner who braved the grind of work for the sake of the family. The home constituted an autonomous area of sovereignty for the housewife and mother, who governed the family's domestic existence. The propensity of the early radical feminists to romanticize work outside the home as exciting or creative, as a place where the average laborer could develop his personality to the full, was noted by G.K. Chesterton early in the century. "These people seem to think," he wrote, "that the ordinary man is a Cabinet Minister. They are always talking about man going forth to wield power, to carve his own way, to stamp his individuality on the world, to command and to be obeyed. . . . Indeed, he is not so free. Of the two sexes the woman is in the more powerful position. For the average woman is at the head of something with which she can do as she likes; the average man has to obey orders and do nothing else. He has to put one dull brick on another dull brick, and do nothing else; he has to add one dull figure to another dull figure, and do nothing else."[21]

If the post-industrial office is characterized by more mobility and more autonomy than the mechanical and regimented drudgery that Chesterton described, it continues to require a high degree of specialization of skills. And it is the specialization of professional work that was always thought by the proponents of "separate spheres" as a narrowing of personality. George Gilder maintains that male rhetoric which gives an inflated importance to marketplace accomplishments and trivializes nonmarket work is really something of a defense mechanism meant to obscure the considerable sacrifice of personality and fulfillment entailed in specialized work.

> Among men the term *dilettante* is a pejorative. Yet, because the range of human knowledge and experience is so broad, the best that most people can ever achieve, if they respond as whole persons to their lives, is the curiosity, openness, and eclectic knowledge of the dilettante. Most men have to deny themselves this form of individual fulfillment. They have to limit themselves, at great psychological cost, in order to fit the functions of the economic division of labor. Most of them endure their submission to the marketplace chiefly in order to make enough money to sustain a home, to earn a place in the household, to be needed by women.[22]

Though male breadwinners in the era before the large-scale entrance of wives and mothers into the workforce sometimes overemphasized the self-directed "career" aspect of work (money, power, achievement, creativity) and downplayed more fundamental reasons for their marketplace involvement (sacrifice for family and service to others), they retained an awareness of the primacy of the domestic sphere. The example of the full-time mother and homemaker, and the existence of a vital domestic life that valued persons, relationships, stability, and permanence allowed marketplace activity to be seen in its true perspective. Inflated notions of personal fulfillment in a "career" were kept down to earth by the solid reality of meeting family responsibilities with a "job."

Social feminists like Frances Perkins, Mary Anderson, and Florence Kelley dedicated their lives to the proposition that mothers should not be forced to work because of economic necessity. They believed that a mother's primary domestic responsibilities of rearing children and keeping house were already considerable without the added task of bringing money into the family. They understood that the majority of wives and mothers at that time only worked outside of the home to supplement the insufficient income of their husbands, and that they viewed the jobs that they held in the marketplace (usually menial and servile work) as a burden. A new generation of feminists set out to make the marketplace involvement of wives and mothers an emotional, psychological, and even economic necessity, on the theory that a career is a liberation from onerous domesticity— a reversal of priorities and outlook. But as Gilder has pointed out, the bulk of work to be done in the modern workforce, despite dramatic improvements in conditions since the beginning of the century, remains essentially servile. "Nothing that has been written in the annals of feminism," says Gilder, "gives the slightest indication that this is a role that women want or are prepared to perform. The feminists demand liberation. The male role means bondage to the demands of the workplace and the needs of the family."[23]

In essence, what began to happen in the 1960s was a large-scale cultural capitulation to the feminist romanticization of marketplace activity, a glamorization based on a caricature of masculine work values. Charlotte Perkins Gilman's belief—utterly countercultural in her own day—that pursuing a career was the only course for self-respecting women was reiterated in the 1960s to a chorus of agreement. Various things contributed to this agreement, including the echochamber of a mass media hostile to the traditional notion of a sacrosanct, female-dominated domestic sphere, as well as an increasing demand on the part of business for female labor, which opened up career opportunities previously closed to women (legislation played an important role in the breakdown of the sex-segregated job market). In retrospect, we can recognize this as a cultural turning point of the most profound significance, when the old, uneasy balance between domestic and marketplace spheres began to break down, and the main force restraining careerism—namely, stay-at-home mothers—began to join the opposition.

In the wake of that breakdown, with the sharp decline in the status and numbers of full-time mothers and homemakers, the somewhat unsavory aspects of the careerist mentality—an overemphasis on competitiveness, power-climbing, and job prestige or status in the workplace—lost their domestic counterbalance. Whether this change was inevitable or not, it is certainly the case that the cultural shift towards an understanding of work based on personal fulfillment and autonomy became much more pronounced, while the view of work as a means of fulfilling family obligations receded into the background.

A vivid sign of the shift is this: We have largely lost one essential component of the work ethic as it developed historically in the United States—the belief in the importance of making use of the fruit of one's labor to save and invest for the future. In 1947, Adriano Tilgher wrote with prophetic insight that "in the United States of America, the religion of work should seem paradoxically but inevitably to be producing a religion its exact opposite, the religion of recreation, pleasure, and amusement."[24] Today, a whole industry of entertainment has arisen to satisfy the culture of amusement. A study in 1992 showed a substantial shift in the direction of saving in the U.S. between 1962 and 1983, from savings to provide for one's heirs towards savings for future personal consumption.[25] The savings rate itself has fallen dramatically. Between the 1960s and the 1990s, according to the *President's Economic Report*, net savings as a percentage of the Gross Domestic Product fell from 8 percent to 2 percent, while personal savings as a percentage of income fell from 8 percent to 4 percent.[26] In 1998, for the first time since the Great Depression, the savings rate fell into negative figures, which means that Americans actually are spending more than they earn.[27] Lest this somehow be taken to indicate greater generosity on the part of the rising generation, it should be noted that this historic decline in frugality has been simultaneous with the decline in volunteerism and charitable giving noted earlier. While a high rate of spending may fuel a growing economy based on consumption, it raises important questions about the very purpose of that growth. If the economy is to provide a stable financial basis for families, we may very well prefer a slower rate of "growth" and a higher rate of saving to massive spending and high rates of growth.

Other signs abound that consumerism, rather than family stability, is prompting Americans to flee from home to office. Gambling has become perhaps the premier leisure activity of Americans: more money is spent on legal gambling in the United States than on movie theaters, books, amusement park attractions, and recorded music combined. One study estimated that Americans lost 41.9 billion dollars on gambling in 1993 alone.[28] This represents a dramatic cultural change. Consider that one of the most popular forms of gambling, state lotteries, did not even exist before 1964 and that most states began to allow legal gambling only in the 1980s or 1990s.

The gambling boom represents a breed of consumerism that is a complete negation of the older ethic of disciplined hard work, self-denial, and sacrifice to provide against future misfortune that moved an earlier generation to save and invest the fruits of their labor. Perhaps that type of long-term commitment was only possible in the optimistic atmosphere that pervaded a more innocent America. Even more significant is the recent astounding growth of pornography, which has become, far and away, the largest "entertainment" industry in the nation. The expense on pornography is a particularly brutal negation of the notion that wealth exists to make possible the formation and sustenance of families.

But the dynamic here is something larger than evolving personal motivations for working, larger even than the personal consumption and immediate gratification that are increasingly taking precedence over saving for one's family. Trends in individual behavior always take place in a wide social context. Could it be that our present economic policies actually encourage certain types of short-sighted, individualistic behavior, at the expense of longer-term commitments? Are certain business practices and individual styles of life rewarded at the expense of others? Who is prospering under the current system, and why?

$\sim$ 4 $\sim$

Making It

*Americans have seen the intimate economics of
their family living fundamentally reordered,
with scant debate and even less awareness of the
consequences for themselves, their children,
and generations to come.*

—Allan Carlson

THE LAST DECADE has been an enormously profitable one for American business. In the 1990s alone, corporate profits doubled, while the stock market tripled in value. One might naturally conclude that American workers—and the families they support—have benefited from all this prosperity, just as they have in previous periods of economic expansion.

Though married women, and particularly married mothers with young children, are working outside the home in ever larger numbers, the income of the average household has remained remarkably stagnant. Median family income in 1997 was a mere 0.6 percent higher than it was in 1989, despite the continued sharp rise in the proportion of dual-income families and in the hours of working wives over this period.[1] How can this be?

A closer look at the income data shows that some workers and some families are keeping ahead of inflation, but many others are losing ground. Most economists tell us that in the new competitive economic order—where unskilled labor is no longer at a premium—it is the level of education that is the primary determinant of earning capacity. But while it is true that after 1980 wages have fallen most drastically for men with a high school education or less, this doesn't tell the entire story. In the median and below median household, average levels of education are up among both women and men, with the number of high school degrees double what it was in 1969 and the number of college degrees up by a factor of almost four. According to the conventional analysis, these workers should be earning more. But they are not. One factor alone seems to explain why the median family struggles to keep its head above water even though wives have substantially upped their work effort. When analyzed from the perspective of the traditional, single-income family and the family wage championed by social feminists like Florence Kelley, Mary Anderson, and Francis Perkins, the past twenty-five years have been an unmitigated disaster.

Since 1973, the median income of men working full-time has declined by about 13 percent, while the median income for women working full-time has climbed by 13.7 percent.[2] The so-called "wage gap" between men's and women's earnings is still a favorite issue of feminist activists, but recent studies have shown that when controlled for demographic and job characteristics, women's earnings are now 92 percent of men's; among younger working women who have never had a child, they approach 100 percent.[3] In fact, the only reason that the median family income hasn't fallen precipitously in the last quarter-century is that wives are working more, and earning more, than ever before. In recent years, as economist Lester Thurow has pointedly said, "the median American female came to the economic rescue of the median American male."[4] In other words, the median American wife came to the economic rescue of the median American family.

But at what cost to family stability, to children, to the social fabric? The older ideal of the family wage championed by social feminists held that the husband should be able to support the average-sized family on a single income, without the wife and mother having to enter the paid labor force. The family-wage concept had always rested on the belief that it was of the utmost importance to free married mothers from the need to supplement the family income because working for pay would force them to neglect their indispensable role in the rearing of children. As Mary Anderson of the Women's Bureau put it, if "the provider for the family got sufficient wages, married mothers would not be obliged to go to work to supplement an inadequate income for their families."[5] By the time those mothers began to enter the workforce in significant numbers in the 1960s, the family wage seemed a permanently established social achievement in the United States, paid by an extraordinary 65 percent of all employers and by more than 80 percent of major industrial employers.[6] In truth, the beginning of the mass exodus of those mothers toward the workplace was more a result of the marked decline in the belief that the female role in rearing and forming children is unique and indispensable than it was the result of increases in the financial pressure on single-earner families. The new feminists had succeeded in convincing married mothers that the traditional belief in the unique capability of women—psychological, physical, and emotional—in the vital task of forming and rearing children was simply part of the male conspiracy to hold them back from genuine fulfillment.

Economic Pressures

But the past twenty-five years have seen an entirely different dynamic at work. Falling earnings for men and the disappearance of the family wage are now having a profound effect on the domestic and professional decisions of married couples in the United States. Ironically, this has occurred precisely at a time when married women in the workforce have begun to express a profound disillusionment with the whole notion of "liberation though career." In the 1980s, the proportion of working mothers who said that they would prefer to be home with the children if it were economically feasible jumped from 33 percent to 56 percent and has remained at approximately that level ever since. Americans now assert, by a margin of two to one, that they would prefer to be a part of a one-earner couple rather than a two-earner couple. A solid majority of mothers working full-time now say that they would rather be working part-time or not at all.[7] That this significant change in attitude toward the workplace was occurring at a time when the percentage of working mothers—particularly those with young children—continued to skyrocket indicates that family finances are an increasingly important element in the decision of mothers to work.

Those who would deny that financial pressure has contributed significantly to the choice of married mothers to enter the paid workforce have pointed out that the increase in the percentage of working moms has been greatest among the wives of top-earning males. This would scarcely be the case, they contend, if economic pressure were a determining factor in the decision to work. But they fail to take into account that as the family wage ceases to be the statistical norm, prices are adjusted to dual-income family standards across the income spectrum. In an economy where the family wage is paid by most employers, one would expect to find the highest percentage of working wives among the families of lower-earning husbands, where supplemental income would make the biggest difference. This was indeed the case as recently as 1969.[8] As median family income falls below the family-wage standard and prices for family commodities begin to reflect a dual-income standard, one would expect the need for supplemental family income to be distributed more evenly across the husbands' income spectrum, even among the wives of median- and high-earning husbands—which is precisely what has occurred.[9] It is also true that wives of high-earning husbands are likely to be high-earners themselves, to have greater career ambitions, and to express considerably less concern about the adequacy of their children's child care arrangements compared to married mothers who are not so well off.

Economic necessity, or perceived economic necessity, is clearly looming larger in the work decisions of married mothers today than it did twenty years ago. While an increasing number express regret at not being able to spend more time with their children, it is not at all clear that their discontent is based on a belief that their children are suffering from their absence. On the contrary, most working mothers seem to remain convinced—despite accumulating empirical evidence and against the traditional wisdom of Western civilization—that their children can get along fine without a more or less constant maternal presence in the home.

But even if the traditional belief that the presence of mothers in the home is essential for the normal development of children (especially young children) were to somehow reestablish itself in the popular culture, the economic aspect of the matter remains unsettled. Is it too late to reestablish the single-income family as an economic norm? The demographic trends and financial incentives operating on the family have now enabled advocates of working mothers to argue that the decision to be a full-time homemaker and mother is not only a socially worthless choice, but an economically unviable one as well.

Increasingly, the decision of married women to raise a family at home is becoming, if not strictly unviable, then certainly economically disadvantageous. As the cost of living rises and male wages fall, the option of married mothers to stay out of—or leave—the paid workforce seems to recede, particularly when incomes and opportunities for working women are on the rise. Even if we restrict our view to the roaring 1990s, the financial cost to families in which the wife chooses to focus her efforts on home and children has become significantly steeper, with the median family income of those families falling by 3.5 percent compared with a rise of almost 5 percent for families in which the wife works.[10]

To put it another way, traditional families have been losing economic ground compared with the new feminist model of dual-income families. In 1989 the median income of the traditional family was still 99.9 percent of the median income for all families; today, it has fallen to 94 percent.[11] In the meantime, families in which the wife chooses to enter the workforce maintained a steady 126 percent of the median family income over this same period.

The spreading income gap between traditional and dual-income families is even more dramatic when one looks at how the market is adjusting itself to the realities of the new domestic economy. Allan Carlson of the Howard Center has shown that between 1970 and 1988 the cost of housing for families where the wife is not in the paid labor force rose by 64 percent relative to income, compared with much smaller 38 percent increase for families with working wives, and he maintains that similar "shifts in the terms of trade" to the disadvantage of single-earner families could be plotted for other consumer commodities.[12] Carlson calculated that as recently as 1976, 40 percent of all jobs still paid enough to support a family of five in minimal comfort; by 1987 only 25 percent of jobs paid such a wage. And in the 1990s, the decline in the purchasing power of traditional, single-earner families has continued unabated. In 1989, for example, the income of the traditional family was 98.5 percent of that of typical married householders; today it is just 88.6 percent of that median.[13]

In short, it is becoming more difficult for the traditional single-income family to afford the normal and necessary expenses of family life. Single-income families, in addition, lag far behind dual-income families in the accumulation of money-measured wealth, the kind that can be saved in bank accounts or invested. It is not going too far to say that dual-income families constitute America's new aristocracy:

whereas in 1969 dual-income families made up only 41 percent of married-couple families with incomes over one hundred thousand dollars, today they make up 98 percent of that category.[14]

Further empirical confirmation of the demise of the family wage is provided by Carlson, who has devised a measure by which to gauge how closely an economy approximates that ideal. The "family wage ratio" is calculated by dividing the median family income of those families with wives in the paid labor force by the median income of those in which the wife is not in the paid labor force. A family wage economy would approach 1.0 while an economy of "pure gender equality" would tend toward 2.0. Carlson found that the ratio remained steady at around 1.25 between 1951 and 1969; since then it has risen sharply to a ratio of about 1.75 today. And single income families, notes Carlson, are, on average, larger and have more dependent children than dual-earner families, which makes the per-capita income deficit even more acute.[15]

Samuel Gompers of the American Federation of Labor described the family wage as "a living wage—which when expended in an economic manner shall be sufficient to maintain an average-sized family in a manner consistent with whatever the contemporary local civilization recognizes as indispensable to physical and mental health."[16] This notion of the family wage is already viewed by most Americans as a quaint, even if desirable, anachronism. Once regarded by social feminists and other progressives as the hallmark and goal of a humane economy which values women and mothers, and a social reality in the United States between the end of the Second World War and the early 1970s, the family wage is now effectively dead.

THE DESTRUCTION OF THE FAMILY WAGE

What accounts for the demise of the family wage in the United States over the past twenty-five years? Apostles of purist free-market economics might maintain that the market is simply accommodating the choices of individuals; that since the late 1960s married women have chosen to enter the workforce in ever increasing numbers and that this private reality is reflected in the fact that single-income families now, necessarily, find the going considerably tougher. The market, they would maintain, simply follows demographics.

There is, certainly, an element of truth to the idea that the market has adjusted to the enormous influx of married women into the workforce over the past quarter-century, both in the sense that that influx has contributed to the precipitous decline in the average wage for men, and because the price of family necessities now reflects an economy in which most wives work. By no means, however, does it fully explain the family wage's demise.

For one thing, while the rise in the proportion of married women in the paid workforce continued steadily throughout the 1950s and 1960s, the wage gap between men and women actually increased and the family wage held firm during that whole period. The family wage ratio only began its steep ascent in the 1980s when single income families began to lose ground more quickly. As Carlson points out, there were factors considerably more relevant to the death of the family wage than simply the rising proportion of working wives. He argues compellingly that the family wage was effectively abolished as a result of three distinct changes in policy: 1) the dismantling of legal barriers to women's employment (protective legislation) and the phasing out of direct wage discrimination (unequal pay for equal work) against female workers in the 1940s; 2) the collapse in the late 1960s of long-standing labor union opposition to wage equality; and 3) the end of job segregation by gender as a result of an amendment to the 1964 Civil Rights Act and its subsequent application by the Equal Employment Opportunity Commission, which had the effect of completely undercutting job discrimination by gender and striking down all state laws granting special protection to women, the very "protective legislation" that social feminists had worked so hard to enact.[17]

The story of the passage of this amendment to the Civil Rights Act of 1964 is fascinating, for it reveals that the key measure used to end sex segregation in the workforce was introduced in an attempt to *prevent* the act from passing. When it became clear in February of 1964 that the Civil Rights act had the number of votes it needed to win passage in the House, Representative Howard J. Smith of Virginia introduced what he considered to be a "killer" amendment, which he judged would be so odious to his fellow members as to ensure the act's defeat. Smith's amendment was aimed at Title VII of the Act which covered "Fair Employment Practices" and prevented discrimination in private employment on the basis of "race, color, religion, or national origin." To this provision, Smith proposed inserting the word "sex," so that women would be counted as another "minority" deserving of special protection from discriminatory employment practices.[18]

The subversive intent behind his move is unquestionable. The previous year, Congress had passed, and President Kennedy had signed, the Equal Pay Act, guaranteeing women the same pay as men for the same jobs. The American workforce, however, remained highly sex-segregated by statute, rule, custom, and social disapproval, and the measure was generally viewed as a sop to quiet the loud new feminists. In highlighting this anomaly—universally accepted in practice as part and parcel of the family-wage regime—Smith and other opponents of civil rights hoped to embarrass liberal supporters of the Civil Rights Act by demonstrating that their opposition to discrimination in employment was inconsistent and hypocritical.[19]

Instead, what he did was to spur the few feminists in the House to action. Although Smith was opposed in his effort to defeat the bill by the Act's principal liberal sponsors and by those most interested in its passage, Representatives Martha Griffiths and Katharine St. George—influenced by the recent trends in feminist thought—latched on to Smith's amendment as a way of breaking down the *de facto* sex segregation of the labor force. Instead of being shamed by Southern segregationists into voting against the Civil Rights Act, liberals in Congress were shamed by the feminists into voting *for* the "killer" amendment. When the act passed, only the Dixiecrats who had introduced the "sex" amendment voted against it.[20]

Several female members of Congress opposed incorporating the amendment, and their arguments were in many ways prophetic. Edith Green, a Democrat from Oregon, noted that "there was not one single bit of testimony given in regard to this amendment. There was not one single organization in the entire United States that petitioned either one of these committees to add this amendment to the bill." Green also read from a letter in which the American Association of University Women argued against adopting the amendment, reasoning that it would have the effect of weakening the bill. Tellingly, she alluded to the "maternalist" reasoning behind the protective legislation passed by a previous generation of feminists: "Because of biological differences between men and women, there are different problems which will arise in regard to employment." But Representative Edna Kelly, Democrat of New York, assured her colleagues that "acceptance of the amendment will not repeal the protective laws of the several States."[21] To Smith's astonishment, the amendment easily passed, and eventually had just the result Edith Green feared: it was used to overturn the protective laws of fifty states. It also effectively ended sex segregation of the labor market when EEOC applied the "proportional representation" theory of "minority" hiring to women.[22] If the principle was spurious when applied to racial minorities, proportional representation was ludicrous when applied to women—it implied that only when women represented half of the workforce in any given profession could "discrimination" be discounted, with no acknowledgment that women devoted to the domestic realm are not even *pursuing* careers.

This policy element in the destruction of the family wage is important to note because it indicates that the achievement and maintenance of a family-wage economy were due not simply to accidental market tendencies but to conscious, or unconscious, policy decisions. Even if it is universally agreed that restoring wage discrimination or job segregation based on gender is both impracticable and inadvisable, this does not mean that the family wage could not itself be restored by other means if such a goal were considered desirable.

In light of the extraordinary trends over the past forty years, it is highly unlikely that single-income families with the wife at home will once again become the statistical norm anytime in the near future. In 1950, two out of three American families fit on the traditional pattern of breadwinning father and mother at home with one or more children; today only one in six families fit that pattern.[23] A cultural milestone was passed around 1982 when, for the first time on record, the percentage of dual-career couples exceeded the percentage of married couples in which the wife did not work. In other words, for families with a husband of working age, full-time dual career couples became the predominant type of family in the early 1980s, outnumbering both families in which the wife worked part-time and families in which the wife stayed home. Full-time dual-career couples now outnumber couples in which the wife does not work by two to one, a complete reversal of the proportions that obtained just twenty-five years ago. Even more astounding is the fact that dual-income married couples without kids (DINKS) now outnumber single-income families with children, which had constituted the most common family type until the mid-1970s.[24]

Though surveys suggest that most Americans still favor more traditional domestic arrangements, since it is no longer the statistical norm (it is, in fact, vastly outnumbered by the number of dual-income families with children) the hope that the traditional model of the single-income married couple with children will return to its former cultural dominance through some sort of natural market preference for strong, stable families is misguided at best. If anything, pure market incentives would tend to favor the DINKS: children, after all, are an increasingly bad bargain for parents in an era of soaring education costs and diminishing financial benefits of having children. One government calculation estimated that the direct cost of raising a child to age eighteen has risen by 20 percent since 1960—and this measure fails to take into account the "forgone wages" of a parent who takes time off to raise their children. The woman who interrupts her career to bear a child can expect to earn less than half as much during her lifetime as the woman who keeps working. *U.S. News and World Report* recently estimated that "the typical child in a middle-income family requires a 22-year investment of just over $1.45 million," an enormous amount for the median income family pulling in forty-one thousand dollars a year.[25] This makes it all the more striking that DINKS enjoy the highest incomes of any family type, whereas the median net worth of couples with children is only about half as high.[26] It may seem in bad taste to say it, but the conclusion is inescapable: Children can do serious damage to a married couple's bank account.

It is becoming increasingly apparent that an economy that makes no distinctions according to relative family responsibilities (that is, between the married earner with five dependents and the single earner with none) will necessarily favor, in many respects, those with fewer responsibilities. This raises the question of whether those who take on greater family or community obligations are putting themselves at an insurmountable disadvantage by handicapping their opportunities at advancement or success in a given line of work, in comparison with colleagues whose lives are more work-centered. Because many firms increasingly value mobility—and equate time spent at the office with loyalty or productivity—employees with family obligations can be at a disadvantage, not simply because they are in direct competition with those who do not have the same economic responsibilities, but also because many corporations actually *prefer* those with fewer obligations at home to distract them from work. Not only do they have the advantage of fewer dependents, but they usually have fewer demands on their time and energy outside the workplace, as well as fewer ties to their community. In an environment where those who can consistently work late hours and are willing to travel or move frequently have a distinct advantage over those who cannot or will not, these are important considerations.

"FAMILY FRIENDLY" BUSINESS

The family-wage economy that prevailed from 1945 to 1970 was the product of an ideal pursued deliberately, primarily by women's organizations, through the political process, in conscious opposition to market incentives tending to draw married mothers out of the home and into the workplace. Today, even if the employment of married women outside the home were to remain at its current level (the highest in our history), this does not mean that it would be impossible to reestablish some degree of economic protection for married mothers who wish to stay at home and raise their children.

It is important to recognize, however, that the initiative for reestablishing a family-wage economy will not come from American corporations or business interests, who have been the primary beneficiaries of our vast social experiment in dual-income families. From the beginning of the industrial age, wives and mothers have been in demand in the workforce as a source of cheaper labor, and it was only through the efforts of labor unions and women's organizations in the late nineteenth and early twentieth centuries that the family wage system was constructed to prevent factory work from claiming more than one family member. In combination with the protective legislation discussed earlier, the family or "living" wage—which formed such an important part of the agenda of the labor movement until the Second World War—had the effect of limiting industry's intrusions into the home.

Among the most consistent and vociferous opponents of the family-wage regime, with its special legal protections for women and children, were industrialists and manufacturing interests who ardently desired to exploit these cheap sources of labor. The National Association of Manufacturers (NAM)—quite representative of industrial interests—publicly campaigned against protective legislation such as mothers' pensions, wage and hour laws, and other laws designed to protect mothers from the necessity of wage work. The arguments used by business interests such as NAM in opposing family-wage legislation, like those of radical feminist allies such as Charlotte Perkins Gilman, were strongly dependent on free market conceptions of the individual's absolute right to contract employment: "The social and material welfare of all classes of people is dependent upon the full exercise of individual freedom consistent with the equal rights of all." NAM argued that "no limitation should be placed upon the opportunities of any person to learn any trade to which he or she may be adapted."[27] Indeed, the chief forces behind the failed attempt to enact the original Equal Rights Amendment in the early part of the century were industrialists and radical women's groups like the National Women's Party. And it was this same odd coalition of radical feminists and business interests that applauded the eleventh-hour perversion of the Civil Rights Act of 1964 into a tool for dismantling the family-wage system.

It is instructive to observe that in the economic expansion after World War II as the labor market tightened, the question of how to draw more women, particularly married women, into the workforce was discussed frequently and fervently by corporate leaders. In 1949 a Royal Commission on Population in Great Britain, made up primarily of prominent business leaders, reported that restrictions on the contributions women could make to economic life were harmful to society; corporate spokesmen in the United States followed this lead in a 1961 Commission on the Status of Women called by President Kennedy, characterizing the more efficient and effective use of women's skills "a necessity."[28] Thus did corporate interests anticipate new feminists like Betty Friedan in their endorsement of the dual-income family model as an economic, if not an ideological, imperative.

One striking historical exhibit is the transcript of the previously-mentioned 1957 conference on "Work in the Lives of Married Women," which brought together U.S. economists, business leaders, and government representatives to discuss the question of how to use the labor—at that time still largely potential—of married women. James P. Mitchell of the Labor Department told the conference that he believed the U.S. could not "continue to advance our standard of living without the integration of women in greater numbers into the work force." Because manpower problems and needs would only become more acute in the coming years, claimed Mitchell, the "farsighted employer" will "have to employ women in ever-increasing numbers and in an increasing variety of jobs." He proposed that the challenge of utilizing the labor of women to the greatest extent possible would require a concerted effort on the part of "employers and the schools, if we are to provide the kind of education and training which are necessary for the attainment of this objective." It would also require reconfiguring existing patterns of full-time employment in order to accommodate the preference of women for part-time work. "If we are to use the woman-power of this country to a greater extent," Mitchell recommended, "we must, among other things, consider how we can use this potential work force by employing women in new and different ways and patterns of work, and in different kinds of jobs."[29]

Mitchell, we now know, underestimated the possibilities of exploiting the potential workforce of married women of childbearing age (he assumed that during these years, "the employer is certain to find himself running a poor second to biology"). But he proved remarkably prescient in predicting the future direction that employment practices would take after gender segregation in the job market and protective legislation came to an end with the EEOC's aggressive implementation of the gender provisions of the 1964 Civil Rights Act. With reference to the reform of educational institutions to "provide the type of education and training necessary for women to be better prepared for careers in the labor force," the revolution has been complete: in 1960, women received only 2.7 percent of all professional degrees awarded and just 10.5 percent of all doctorates; today they receive 38.5 percent of all professional degrees and 40.7 percent of all doctorates.[30] The gender desegregation of the nation's institutions of higher learning and professional schools by academic administrations ideologically bent on ending the economic dependence of married women on their husbands took place at roughly the same time as the gender desegregation by law of the professions; both were necessary components of eliminating the family-wage regime.

In a recent "Survey of Women and Work," the *Economist* magazine summarized some of the advantages to employers of an expanded labor pool in which the great majority of married women work. One is that as the formerly nonmonetary functions of the household are commercialized, new markets are created: "Being able to draw on a larger pool of available workers improves the quality of labor, reduces the risk of shortages and raises demand, not least for goods and services that will make a working woman's life easier: labor-saving devices, convenience foods, meals out, child care." The article goes on to list some of the reasons employers find female labor particularly attractive, all of which tend to undermine the job market for those attempting to support a family on a single wage: "In America, with its booming economy and tight labor market, women are proving a godsend to many employers. They usually cost less to employ than men, are more prepared to be flexible and less inclined to kick up a fuss if working conditions are poor. . . . Employers like them because they allow more flexibility and command lower pay, and because part-timers can be pushed harder while they are at work."[31] All this is seen by the laissez-faire *Economist* as a welcome development that allows employers to economize on labor costs and compete in the global economy. Absent from their considerations is any thought of how this affects the employee trying to support a family.

Seen in this light, "family friendly" policies (such as more liberal leave provisions and on-site day care) clearly work to the advantage of companies that wish to retain, or attract, married mothers. Companies admit as much. In 1989, former British Prime Minister Margaret Thatcher encountered stiff opposition from business when she encouraged mothers to stay at home with their young children (which she regarded as a key to solving the increasing problem of violent, anti-social behavior by British youth). Employers complained that a scarcity of women in the labor market would help to push up wages, and British corporations responded by providing more liberal maternity leave with guaranteed reemployment. In addition, companies introduced new incentives that would wean mothers from their babies and get them back to work, such as 25-percent pay raises for the six months after maternity leave, reserving payment until after the mother returned to work.[32]

Although usually not as explicit about their intentions, American companies, of course, have similar motivations behind "family friendly" policies. Johnson & Johnson has determined that they are saving four dollars in increased productivity and retraining costs for every dollar expended on their Life Works maternity-leave and child care program. Randall Tobias, chairman and chief executive of Eli Lilly was recently quoted as saying that he did not consider his company's expanded family leave programs to be employee benefits, so much as tools that "will help us attract, motivate and retain people who are more likely to be dedicated, more focused, more innovative and more productive." Such "family friendly" policies have the additional benefit of giving larger corporations a competitive advantage over their smaller competitors, who are often unable to afford such benefits—or tools.

According to one recent estimate, about eight thousand companies in the United States now offer on-site day care, up from only two hundred in 1982.[33] And American corporations, always on the cutting edge of innovation for the sake of efficiency, are going to new extremes to accommodate mothers of young children. Patagonia, an outdoor-clothing company in California, offers mothers a fully accredited on-site kindergarten, "lactation-support" services (which means that mothers are allowed to bring their infant children into meetings so as not to miss a scheduled breast-feeding), and after-school care for older children, maintaining that these perks are cost-effective because they reduce turnover and absenteeism. In recent years, pediatricians have insisted on the importance of breast-feeding for infants in the first year after birth, citing growing evidence that the practice reduces the risk of diarrhea, ear infections, allergies, and sudden infant death syndrome, as well as the risk to women of ovarian and breast cancer. As a result, almost three hundred American employers, including Aetna, Eastman Kodak, Cigna, and Home Depot, now offer "lactation support rooms" where female employees can take regular breaks to attach electric pumps to their breasts in order to collect the milk in bottles for their infants in day care. Some companies, aside from the "pumping rooms," have "lactation consultants" to help mothers solve breast-feeding problems. Aetna, one such company, estimates that it saves $1,435 and three days of sick leave per breast-fed baby—a three to one return on their investment.[34]

In fact, family friendly policies are now considered a top priority by "human resource" professionals in the corporate world, essential for any company that wishes to stay competitive. A 1996 conference sponsored by the Family and Work Institute in New York City highlighted some of the benefits that the more "progressive" companies are now offering, including domestic-partner benefits for same-sex couples, described by Andrew Sherman, vice president of the Segal Company, as a "win-win" strategy for employers who gain a reputation for "enlightened" policies at a minimal cost. Some companies, such as Lotus, actually restrict domestic partner benefits to same-sex couples only, on the theory that opposite-sex couples already receive benefits by law through marriage. Christian Kjeldsen of Johnson & Johnson pointed to the popularity of his company's on-site day care centers, noting that the center located at the corporate headquarters had two hundred children and a growing waiting list. The company's day care program, he said, was not a response to employee demand, but to several articles in business magazines on the changing demographics of the job market; Kjeldsen maintained that such benefits would be a permanent fixture despite recent downsizing and "early-outs" at the company. In other words, Johnson & Johnson has judged it more cost-effective to warehouse the young children of some employees than to retain the jobs of others whose incomes may be providing for their families without recourse to day care. Family friendly benefits do not, as it turns out, include job security.[35]

And family friendly policies emphatically do not include paying one parent enough to support a family on a single income. That "outdated" view of the family, argued Randall Tobias of Eli Lilly, is why some companies' antiquated personnel policies are still "based on Ozzie and Harriet." Because such traditional family structures only apply to about 18 percent of employees in the U.S., according to Tobias, companies need to take on an increasingly paternal role. Eli Lilly, in addition to on-site day care, has a cafeteria that prepares take-home dinners four nights a week, a dry cleaning facility, and a twenty-four hour counseling service for its employees. Tobias emphasizes the bottom-line benefits the company reaps from such progressive policies: "the child care facility," he asserted, "will benefit not only the families that use it, but all our employees, stockholders, customers— all who benefit from the undivided attention of our employees." Because of increased conflict at home and family-related stress, many companies, such as Marriott in Atlanta, have begun to offer professional counseling from a staff of full-time social workers. Human Resources Director Donna Klein explained that Marriott decided to retain social workers on staff because some managers were spending an inordinate amount of their time counseling employees with family problems.[36]

This new paternalist attitude on the part of U.S. corporations was justified by Robert Allen, CEO of AT&T, in the following words, featured in the promotional literature of the Family and Work conference: "We have not traditionally linked the well-being of children to the success of business or the governance of nations. Yet increasingly we're acknowledging that upheavals in the American family aren't self-contained—they intersect with business and economic circles and loop into the social fabric of this nation. As a society, we assume a large affiliation—one that implies, not just family ties, but added obligations."[37]

What is so striking about Mr. Allen's formulation is that the well-being of children is accorded importance insofar as it affects "the success of business or the governance of nations." This reflects a reversal of the concern with an expanding commercialism that the family-wage regime was erected to guard against: the intrusion into the domestic sphere of industrial or business pressures, to the detriment of family welfare. It tells us that we have experienced a true cultural revolution in the relationship of work and family. The question is now whether "upheavals in the American family" impinge on the success of business rather than whether the success of business impinges on the sanctity of the family.

Dependent Independence

To regard the family as a potential or actual impediment to the normal and efficient functioning of business is to echo the new feminism of the 1960s. One of the central contentions of Friedan and her followers was that the family obligations of women need not put them at any greater disadvantage in the workplace than those of men, and motherhood should not be regarded by working women or their employers as a significant barrier to a full-time effort on the career track. Hence the redefinition of pregnancy as a "sickness," which eventually won legal recognition requiring companies to treat pregnancy as a "disability" no different from any other.

The irony is that the new feminism, which began in an attempt to achieve the economic independence of women from men, has only succeeded in achieving a new dependence on two incomes for those families that might prefer to have the mother at home with the children. Now that the family wage has been effectively destroyed, that option is no longer a possibility for many American families. And the promise of financial independence as a result of the abolition of the sexual division of labor has proved elusive: the so-called "femininization of poverty" amounts to the realization that without the income of a husband, most single mothers find it difficult if not impossible to make ends meet, something any of the old social feminists could have told them. As British sociologist Geoff Dench put it several years ago, "equal opportunity policies seem to be accompanied by growing female poverty, and women's dreams of financial independence via the market are turning to dust."[38]

Emancipation from financial dependence on wage-earning husbands has also led to the new dependence on seemingly paternalistic corporations to provide "benefits" such as day care. And the family functions of the paternal organization do not end at child care provisions for employees; they now include training in values and behavior as well. In *Time Bind*, Arlie Hochschild relates an amazing list of courses offered by one of the corporations she studied, which includes *Dealing with Anger, How to Give and Accept Criticism, How to Cope with Difficult People, Stress Management, Taking Control of Your Work Day, Improving Team Effectiveness, Work-Life Balance,* and *Self-Awareness and Being.* Modern corporations are beginning to take on family functions as fundamental as the formation of character, things that would have been regarded as off-limits a generation ago.[39] But as the private realm of the domestic ceases to function in fulfilling fundamental human needs, the paternal corporation steps in today with little protest.

The increasingly clamorous demand for further public subsidies of day care for the children of working mothers would simply be one more step along the road of institutionalizing the dual-income family, the cost of which subsidization would be disproportionately borne by single-income families who would share in none of the benefits. Completely unjustifiable from the standpoint of relative income, this subsidization of working mothers is eminently logical from the perspective of modern feminist ideology: subsidized day care would be, in effect, the ultimate cultural endorsement of the idea that a mother's place is in the office and that her presence in the home is of little importance—that it is, in fact, undesirable.

Similarly, new government regulations requiring businesses to provide more liberal family leave or day care for employees converge with the interests of larger corporations, who have little to lose from further government mandates. Bigger businesses can easily absorb the cost, and retain the loyalty of married-mother workers at the same time, while smaller competitors sink under the regulatory burden. The situation calls to mind Hilaire Belloc's prediction early in the century that the threat to freedom in the West was not from socialism per se, but from an unholy alliance of big government and big business, wherein the security of workers would be guaranteed by means of government regulation, confirming the economic dominance of larger corporations.[40] Governments, too, have a direct interest in subsidizing the dual-income regime through mandated "family friendly" benefits. Maximizing the number of married women in the work force also means maximizing Social Security payments and income tax revenues, which will help to pay for the rapidly growing number of retired people.

But the short-sightedness of such policies is apparent. Having withdrawn their support from the traditional family, America's corporations may very well find that they have undermined the source of productive, responsible, and trustworthy workers. The traditional family is a source of motivation for effort and excellence at work, rather than a source of anxiety that impinges on a worker's ability to focus on the job and requires ever more company resources to deal with family problems that ought to be solved at home. In subsidizing working mothers, government may maximize taxable income in the short term, but such a policy can only further aggravate the problem of declining fertility at the root of the social security "crisis"—which is essentially a demographic crisis, not a financial one.

Surveys seem to indicate a growing sense among many Americans that their lives are becoming all too centered around the workplace, while home-related concerns, especially children, could benefit from a good deal more attention. There is growing disillusionment among working mothers with the daily grind of office life and the burden of trying to be both breadwinner and primary caregiver to children. But while polls show that more time with their families is at the top of the agenda of most working mothers, government policy is headed in the opposite direction, with tax, child care, and family-leave policies aimed at keeping mothers on the career track.

This is, in part, because the economic policies of both liberals and conservatives are aimed at procuring and sustaining "growth" rather than sustaining the family. But economic growth unmoored from the primary unit of society, the family, is at best a value-neutral concept. The success of some of the biggest "growth" industries of recent decades—such as day care and fast food—can be regarded as a measure of the decline of domestic life, and yet these industries can contribute significantly to overall economic growth. What economists term economic growth depends, to a large degree, on the transfer to the commercial economy of functions formerly performed in the nonmonetary domestic sphere. In this sense, using growth of the Gross Domestic Product, for example, as a measure of economic health is deceptive; it tells us nothing about how easy it is for families to build a domestic life set aside from the forces of the marketplace. If mere growth is the goal of economic policy, then the family can be seen as a positive impediment to achieving that aim because familial bonds impede the optimal allocation of labor and domestic productivity limits the influence of the commercial economy. If, on the other hand, family life is precisely what the economy exists to serve, then it follows that the prevalence of the family wage, rather than mere growth, is the appropriate measure of economic well-being for any society.

In fact, the experience of the past two decades strongly indicates that economic growth has a negative effect on the fertility of married women in an economy where the dual-earner couple is the statistical norm. And if we believe that the reason for the family's existence is to form and raise the next generation of citizens, workers, producers, and—not least—mothers and fathers, this outcome has profoundly disturbing social, as well as economic, implications.

An Outline of Sanity

The family is thus the key to a healthy society and its economy. If the family flourishes, society will be sound. But this is a reciprocal process: the family cannot survive without a good economy, and society cannot survive without good families. Nevertheless, the economy must serve the family because the family does not exist to serve the economy. The family is and will be fundamental to the economic organization of society.

—Conference on "The Family and Economy in the Future of Society"

ONE BY ONE, the pillars that supported the family-wage economy have been knocked down. They had been designed to enable the single-earner family to subsist comfortably and to allow that family to raise children within the home. The pillars had been three: protective legislation, enacted after concerted effort on the part of the vast network of women's organizations wishing to protect mothers from the necessity of paid employment and children from neglect; wage discrimination in favor of male heads of families, procured by labor unions at the height of their prestige and power; and gender segregation of the workforce, a product of both cultural habit and the aforementioned protective legislation. By the late 1970s, each of these supports had been destroyed—by conscious effort on the part of a feminist and business elite and neglect on the part of a comfortable society that had ceased to see any need to shield the home and the family from destructive market and state pressures.

Today, reconstructing such a system is scarcely conceivable. The social forces primarily responsible for constructing the family-wage economy—labor unions and grass-roots women's organizations dedicated to the domestic ideal—have lost the political influence and cultural dominance they once possessed, and the social forces unalterably opposed to such a regime are now more powerful than ever. The New Feminist ideology of equal opportunity and full female participation in the professions, regarded as radical just forty years ago, is today a given, seen by most people as an issue of fundamental equity and a prerequisite for any just society. Perhaps even more important, a consensus of opposition to federal and state regulation of wages and employment (with the exception of minimum-wage laws) now spans the political spectrum as never before. Direct intervention by the state in the ability of employers to set wages is regarded by both conservatives and liberals as a violation of one of the fundamental elements of the free-market economy necessary to the prosperity and efficiency of a free society. The inefficiency and injustice that result from governmental regulation of wages and prices are acknowledged by both Left and Right as ingredients in a recipe for economic disaster.

A strong argument could be made, even by family-wage advocates, that these changes are mostly for the good. The duty of society to maintain a "preferential option for the family"—to ensure that the choice of those married mothers and families wishing to follow the traditional pattern is not punished by undue social or financial burdens—need not require punishing those women who want to pursue careers by erecting legal or regulatory barriers to their advancement.

This is not to say that government has no role to play in the modern economy. It is particularly important in the era of the new "globalized market" that governments protect the rights of workers and their representatives against exploitation by large business concerns. But even the most ardent union supporters would acknowledge that the setting of wage rates or ratios by government according to profession or class of worker would lead to inefficiencies and injustices. State planned or managed economies have been among the most thoroughly discredited ideas of the twentieth century.

Short of reconstructing the family-wage regime along the lines of the now-abandoned model, are there other ways of creating the same "preferential option" for the family at which the older policies aimed? The standard idea of most conservative and "pro-family" advocates on the political scene today is to reduce the crushing tax burden on average families, which has increased so sharply in the past fifty years. The statistics bear out this contention: due largely to the loss in value of the personal exemption for children, the effective federal income tax rate for the average family of four has gone from about 3 percent in 1948 to almost 25 percent today.[1] In 1948 the personal exemption was equivalent to about 17 percent of the median income for a family of four, so that after exemptions for children and the standard deduction, almost half of working families were subject to no income tax at all. If the personal exemption had kept pace with inflation, it would be over eight thousand dollars today.[2] During the same period, Social Security or payroll taxes went from one percent of that average family's income to almost 8 percent, and state and local taxes rose sharply as well.[3] All told, this family of four is likely to have a total tax burden of over 35 percent of family income.[4]

The essential point is that the changes in the tax system in this period have all been at the expense of traditional families. As George Gilder has noted, "since 1950, all increases in personal taxation have fallen on married couples with children. While mothers of illegitimate children receive massive benefits, and single or 'child free' couples have faced no increase in average taxation, taxes on couples with children have risen between 100 and 400 percent depending on the number of offspring."[5]

Taxing Families

The policy of funding the post-Great Society welfare state with money collected from married couples with children is not accidental. The fateful and unprecedented decision of social planners and policy-makers of the era to allow unmarried mothers to receive benefits under the Aid to Families with Dependent Children (AFDC) program marked what was in retrospect a turning point in social policy, and one which had permanent consequences for the orientation of the federal government toward traditional families. Historically, AFDC was an outgrowth of the Mothers' Pension laws enacted early in the century and federalized during the New Deal. The philosophy behind the program was perfectly consistent with the reinforcement of the traditional family which the entire family-wage regime was designed to accomplish. Roosevelt's administration defended the ADC program when it was introduced in 1935 precisely as a way of keeping mothers at home: "[ADC is] designed to release from the wage-earning role the person whose natural function is to give her children the physical and affectionate guardianship necessary not only to keep them from falling into social misfortune, but more affirmatively to rear them into citizens capable of contributing to society."[6] In fact, aiding widowed mothers, those whose husbands were incapacitated, and those with working husbands unable to meet the family's financial needs provides no financial incentive that undermines the family norm, understood as the single-income married couple with children raised in the home. Benefits provided to supplement the loss of the husband's income due to death, disability, or insolvency assume that norm and have the effect of strengthening incentives to marry and have children rather than weakening them.

Once unmarried mothers are made eligible for benefits, however, the pro-family effect of the system is fundamentally altered. Such a subsidy makes the decision to have a child out of wedlock considerably easier (and with the perverse incentives of the current system, easier to make—in many cases—than having a child within marriage), and it taxes the traditional family to support behavior that directly undermines it. Whether the subsequent huge increase in illegitimacy was a result of this fundamental policy shift is a question that will be debated for years to come; what cannot be denied is that the money to support unmarried mothers has come primarily from married couples with children.

The movement to reform welfare derives in part from a belated recognition that the current system has undermined the traditional family, particularly in the black community, by taxing such families to support behavior fundamentally at odds with traditional morality. A less recognized, but equally important, aspect of the growing tax burden on traditional families over the last forty years has been the marked shift in the system of income tax from a bias in favor of families to a bias in favor of individuals. This is a fundamental point, and one that many inclined to favor alleviating the tax burden on families have not grasped. The question of whether an income tax system tends to tax individual earners or families as a unit is all-important in determining whether that system works to the advantage or disadvantage of families. Like the question of the circumstances under which the state will support indigent mothers, the question of whether a tax system is oriented towards individuals or towards families does not admit of a neutral answer. If the income tax regards families as the fundamental unit, it will work to the detriment of individual earners; if individual earners are taxed, it will work to the detriment of the family.

One recent example of how this principle is not sufficiently grasped by those ostensibly friendly to the cause of the traditional family is the debate among conservatives over the merits of the five-hundred-dollar-per-child tax credit that was part of the "Contract with America." Some of the strongest opposition to the proposal came not from feminists or homosexual rights advocates but from conservative Republicans, who argued that the credit would constitute a subsidy from all taxpayers to some families with children, and hence would be an instance of government unduly interfering in peoples' free choices by encouraging one type of family structure to the exclusion of others.[7] On this theory, the five-hundred-dollar credit is at odds with free-market doctrine, which would maintain that government has no business encouraging a particular type of family; that is the role of the market, which will naturally prefer the most efficient and productive type of family structure according to the "free choice" of individuals.

This argument, of course, conveniently ignores that even the woefully insufficient existing individual deduction is based on an implicit understanding that the bearing and raising of children is an expense which society has the obligation to help families defray, both because children are the next generation of workers, taxpayers, and parents, and because the cost to society will be much greater in the long run if those children are deprived of the benefits of home and family. Perhaps it is the case that the newfound enthusiasm of some conservatives for a "flat tax" on all income, with no allowance for deductions of any type, is an indication that the movement away from taxing families as a unit is more than accidental.

The *Economist*'s survey of "Women and Work" is more forthright about the fundamental opposition between taxing income in a way that acknowledges the family's contribution to the economy and tax-

ing income in a way that is ostensibly "neutral" toward family structure. Acknowledging that the flood of mothers into the workforce has
"involved a big social shift," the *Economist* asserts that the rapid
changes have left "attitudes, norms and institutions behind" which
were "designed for the traditional model of male breadwinner, female
homemaker and child-carer." It recommends that industrialized nations recognize that "the clock cannot be turned back," because "modern economies could not function without women workers, and few
women now would want to function without jobs." Since "the present
system is neither as fair nor as efficient as it might be," the *Economist*
opines, "governments, employers and individuals all need to rethink
their roles." As to the role of governments, "the sort of incentives or
disincentives they offer can make a big difference to the way people
organize their lives. If, for example, the tax system favors the traditional breadwinner-housewife family, fewer women will go out to
work. The same is true of social-security systems. If governments
want women to be able to make a free choice about taking jobs, they
need to tailor tax and social-security systems to individuals rather
than family units."[8]

Here it is that the fallacy of "neutrality' in the tax system and
providing women with "a free choice about taking jobs" is laid bare.
If government decides that it will no longer defray the cost entailed
for families in raising children, this does not so much allow mothers
more freedom of choice in the matter of work as it compels them to
seek paid employment outside the home to supplement insufficient
family income. In a sense, some form of child care will have to be
"subsidized" by the tax code; either government will allow parents to
keep more of their earned income in order to raise their children at
home, or government will face increasing pressure to subsidize day
care for the children of mothers forced into the workplace. The progressive social thinkers at the *Economist* recognize as much when they
admit that "a system that will produce more children and still keep
women at work . . . may not be cheap," and suggest the solution lies

in "subsidizing child care," as well as mandating family and medical leave policies.[9]

The point is that policymakers in the coming years are faced with two choices: either they strengthen the protective barriers around the family because they recognize the benefits to society of keeping children at home with their parents, or they allow those barriers to erode further, which will work to the benefit of those who desire to see more mothers at work and more children in some form of substitute care. Allan Carlson has pointed out that the domestic relations within the family—particularly those between parents and children—are the pre-capitalist foundation stones of the social order, and as such cannot be subjected to the centrifugal forces of the market, in which efficiency and profitability are the sole ordering principles of human relationships.[10] The family remains the only institution that operates on the communist principle of "to each according to his needs, from each according to his ability"; it also remains the only institution positively essential to the very existence of a social order on which all other institutions are based. Again, whether the tax system views this cell of the social organism as indivisible or as subject to division will affect the very life of the body politic.

Recent proposals to eliminate the "marriage penalty" in the tax code underscore the importance of this fundamental distinction. The marriage penalty refers to the extra income tax assessed on some married couples filing jointly, in comparison to what they would have been taxed filing separately as singles. A bill introduced in the House of Representatives in 1998 by Republicans Jerry Weller and David McIntosh proposed to do away with the penalty by allowing married couples to file separately or jointly, depending on which option results in the lower tax rate. The proposed change was supported by over two hundred members of the House, including the Republican leadership, as well as numerous conservative presidential aspirants who emphasize their "family values" agenda.

But the "neutrality" toward marriage of the framers and supporters of this measure is based on the principle of treating all earners as independent entities, a principle fundamentally at odds with treating the family as an economic unit. Ostensibly, a family-friendly bill eliminating a "marriage penalty," the reform would have the effect of creating an additional "homemaker penalty" by further shifting the tax burden onto single-earner couples while reinforcing the marriage-weakening notion that the individual is society's basic unit for purposes of taxation. As originally written, it would have had the same detrimental effects on the family that all reforms of the income tax code have had over the last thirty years: it would have increased the incentive for married mothers to enter the work force, while diminishing incentives to marry and to raise chlidren at home. To their credit, the bill's sponsors were convinced of this and adjusted their proposal accordingly.

TAX "REFORM"

The irony is that the whole issue of eliminating a marriage penalty in the tax code has arisen because of earlier "reforms" wherein legislators similarly ignored the importance of treating the family as a unit. From the introduction of the income tax system in 1913 until 1944, the federal code had disregarded marriage in its assessment of income, and earners were taxed without reference to their marital status. During this entire period, family well-being declined, as divorce rose and the marriage and fertility rates fell. It was only in the 1930s that family structure began to count as a factor in the way federal income tax was assessed, when a Supreme Court decision had the effect of allowing married couples in certain states to "split" the family income in their joint returns, each claiming half of the total income, which meant lower taxes for married couples as a result of the existing progressive rates.[11]

Two tax reforms in the 1940s had the effect of shifting rates dramatically in a pro-family direction. In 1944, Congress created the individual exemption for household members related by blood, marriage, or adoption, amounting to five hundred dollars per person. Four years later, another tax reform act increased the exemption to six hundred dollars and allowed the practice of income-splitting for every married couple in the nation (until that point income-splitting was available only in states with "community property" laws). It all added up to substantial tax breaks for married couples, particularly those with children.[12]

It is not merely coincidental that the years from 1946 through 1964 were, statistically speaking, the best years of the twentieth century for the American family. These were precisely the years of the Baby Boom, when the fertility rate for married couples rose substantially, while the divorce rate dropped, the marriage rate climbed, and the proportion of mothers at home grew. Other factors undoubtedly contributed to the domestic renaissance, but the truly family-friendly features of the tax code during these years had a salutary effect on the positive family trends.

Every subsequent major adjustment in the way federal income tax is assessed has been to the detriment of the family, primarily because legislators lost sight of the central principle that there is no such thing as a "family neutral" income tax. In an attempt to alleviate what was thought to be a disproportionate tax burden on unmarried workers, the Nixon Administration proposed a reform in 1969, subsequently enacted by Congress, that cut rates for singles, while eliminating both income-splitting and the option of filing separately for married couples (this adjustment resulted in the "marriage penalty" for many dual-income couples which lawmakers are attempting to eliminate today, a penalty which became a political liability in subsequent years due to the expanding constituency of dual-income families). Not only that, but the dependent exemption was not adjusted for inflation during this period, a result of complaints by the burgeoning population-control lobby that the tax code was too "pro-natalist"—as if those interested in raising children form some sort of special interest group.[13] It added up to a significant reduction in the economic benefits of marriage and children.

Not surprisingly, the positive family trends of the Baby Boom quickly reversed themselves, with married couple fertility sharply down, the marriage rate falling, and the divorce rate soaring. The proportion of dual-income couples was also sharply up, as both the tax system and the courts ceased to uphold the legal claims of married women to an equal share of husbands' income. The disallowance of income-splitting in the tax code and the trend in "no-fault" divorce rulings combined to undermine the economic security of the housewife and mother with regard to her legal right to an equal share of family income that she did not earn herself.

Another turning point was the Dependent Care Tax Credit passed in the early 1970s, which granted tax relief (today worth almost fifteen hundred dollars per child) only to those working couples who put their children in commercial day care. This truly revolutionary measure was an astounding departure in family policy, and it—like the earlier decision to give direct pubic assistance to unmarried mothers—should be seen as a crucial turning point in the moral consensus that had guided all federal family policy since its inception. Just as using AFDC funds to aid unmarried mothers was the first time that federal tax dollars had been used to support a practice at odds with traditional morality (having children out of wedlock), so the granting of substantial tax breaks specifically to families opting for nondomestic care for their children was a direct attack on the structure of the traditional family. In this case, there is evidence that the Dependent Care Tax Credit was actually conceived as a way of taxing the "nonproductive" work of mothers at home for the benefit of those mothers engaged in "productive" work in the paid labor force.[14] In both cases, more of the tax burden shifted to single-income families who were not only funding programs from which they received no direct benefit, but were also, in effect, made to fund their own destruction.

Proponents have contended that federally-subsidized child care is merely a way of providing mothers with an option to work if they so wish, and is entirely neutral as regards the decision of mothers to raise their children at home or use professionalized day care. George Gilder notes that "far from being a neutral program, even-handedly extending options of motherhood and job, subsidized day care is a massive multibillion dollar federal endorsement of one option—the uninterrupted career." It is, says Gilder, a direct attack on stay-at-home mothers.[15]

The history of child care subsidies in the United States and the stated intentions of the proponents of such measures confirm his contention. One of the earliest state-funded day care programs—California's 3.5 million dollar allocation in 1946—was pushed through the state legislature in a lobbying campaign by social workers and child care specialists, who deceptively used the rhetoric of maternalism to bolster their cause. On the federal level, after the original intentions of the AFDC program had been subverted by granting benefits to unwed mothers, it was but a short step to federally subsidized child care, which was an even more direct blow to the traditional family structure in that it indicated a governmental preference for raising children outside the home.

A hint of what was to come could be gleaned from the 1970 White House Conference on Children, the conclusions of which differed radically from those of its predecessors. Previous gatherings of academics and business representatives had concluded that mothers working outside the home constituted no threat to children in the nuclear family; now it became clear that the agenda was to do away with family norms altogether. Much more politically charged than previous conferences, it included a significant contingent of feminist and civil rights activists bent on overturning long-held assumptions about the family. While the conference report did not attack the traditional family per se, it signaled a fundamental policy shift in its completely relativistic view of the structure of domestic life. We "do not favor any particular family form," the conference delegates wrote. "Children can and do flourish under many other family forms than the traditional nuclear structure."[16]

Feminist delegates explicitly saw the conference as an ideal place to float the notion that professionalized day care was a perfectly adequate alternative to maternal care, with the not-so-ulterior motive of freeing women to pursue careers. In order to emphasize that a mother who chooses to work is not therefore irresponsible, they had to undermine the importance traditionally attributed to caring for children *in the home*. The finished report of the conference did precisely this: "The *place* where care is given," it argued, "is not the most significant dimension for the child. . . . The issue is the kind of care given, how he is handled, what abilities are nurtured, what values are learned, and what attitudes toward people are acquired."[17]   The report also pointed to the advantages that day care presented for the proper socialization of children (to that extent anticipating the whole multicultural movement). "Think for a moment what this would mean," remarked leading feminist delegate Representative Bella Abzug. "It would let local groups of parents and women set up child care centers for children from all socio-economic backgrounds. . . . A child care system that would accommodate rich and poor alike, that would let our kids grow up with a chance to know each other and to learn that they can bridge the racial and economic gap that divides their parents."[18]

The very next year brought a tax reform that allowed substantial deductions for parents using commercialized day care, for the first time actually shifting tax incentives towards nonparental care. Earlier in 1971, Congress had enacted a much more radical day care measure, a "child development" bill that would have mandated attendance at federally-run centers for almost every pre-school child in the United States. It was vetoed by President Nixon, who rightly noted in his veto message that the measure would have the effect of pledging "the vast moral authority of the federal government to the side of communal approaches to childrearing as against a family centered approach."[19] The same logic could have been used just as validly against the tax deductions eventually enacted.

Since then, the trend in government child care policy has been consistently towards subsidizing "professionalized," nonparental, commercial care outside the home at the expense of stay-at-home mothers. In 1976 and again in 1984, Congress significantly increased and expanded tax preferences for child care outside the home. In 1981, it granted a special tax credit to two-income couples, specifically as a way to tax the domestic work of the mother and homemaker that evaded normal IRS measurements of income in the "productive" economy.[20] This marked the first time that the federal government had explicitly asserted the right to tax transactions in the domestic realm, the nonmarket economy of the home that family-wage advocates had fought for so long to defend.

SUBSIDIZING DAY CARE

As mothers have entered the workforce in larger numbers (and as their contribution to family income has become more essential) in the past fifteen years, the pressure to expand federal subsidies of child care has continued, although, interestingly enough, most of the lobbying still comes from the professional day care industry and feminist groups. Even the advocates of day care legislation admit that there has been no groundswell of public sentiment for more federally-supported child care. In reference to the ABC Child Care Bill passed by Congress in 1990 (an expansion of subsidies that was barely defeated in the Senate), Representative George Miller later acknowledged, "I spent eight years in getting the child-care bill passed in Congress, and at its zenith, there was never a child-care movement in the country. There was a coalition of child-advocacy groups, and a few large international unions that put in hundreds of thousands of dollars, and we created in the mind of the leadership of Congress that there was a child-care movement—but there was nobody riding me. And not one of my colleagues believed their election turned on it for a moment."[21] Today a similar coalition is mobilized in support of the child care legislation proposed by President Clinton, a grab-bag of a bill which would expand existing deductions for commercial care while granting new tax breaks to businesses that institute on-site day care for children of employees. Again, there is no groundswell of enthusiasm for the measures outside of the professional child care lobby.

That lack of grassroots pressure to expand day care programs is not surprising when one considers that most working mothers are still opting for at-home care arrangements for their children when they are at work. The surprising thing is that relatively few parents are putting their children in commercial day care, given the incentives that would make that choice more affordable than other options for mothers. Editor and columnist Terence Jeffrey described some of the economic sacrifices that the IRS requires of the married couple that chooses to have the mother raise their children at home. Jeffrey tells of a meeting with a "benefits coordinator" at his workplace, who informed him that the IRS allows employers to "set aside" a portion of the employee's paycheck for certain approved family expenditures; in other words, some income will not be taxed as long as the employee promises to spend the money on "a narrowly limited set of items." Jeffrey writes that "one of the biggest ticket pre-taxable items is something called 'dependent care.' You can sock away up to $5,000 tax free to pay for it." The catch is that Jeffrey's wife, who is raising their four children at home, does not qualify. If his wife wants to hire a baby-sitter for one night a week to take care of the kids in their home, this does not qualify as dependent care. "Why? The government says she spends *too* much time with our kids." He goes on to describe the tax advantages that would accrue to the family from the decision to put the kids in commercial care:

It would be a different story if my wife had decided to hire some professional agency to raise our children so that she could keep the well-paying job she once had managing a small business in downtown Washington.

Indeed, were my wife to go back to work and begin regulating her life according to the financial incentives created by the government—rather than according to the softer stuff that seems to corrupt the economic rationality of full-time moms—she would discover that tax-free baby-sitting is just one of the benefits that would flow to her from a government that understands the hardships of two-income yuppie parenting.

Back on the job, with the kids socked away in daycare somewhere, my wife would be allowed to begin stacking up her own pre-tax 401(k) savings—potentially doubling the wealth of our family after her retirement.

Jeffrey concludes that "the model 20th century American family, as I read the tax code, is two unmarried people, who both work, whose illegitimate children are reared by a government subsidized dependent-care center."[22]

But even with all the enticements to take advantage of government-approved commercial care, most parents have not succumbed, preferring "informal" care arrangements with relatives or neighbors, usually in the home. One likely explanation is that parents understand, despite continuing attempts to downplay the data, that the care provided in these commercial centers is inadequate at best.

This is perhaps why proponents of the Clinton Administration's proposed twenty-two-billion-dollar expansion of child care funding are pushing it with a tried-and-true method: they use traditional-family rhetoric to encourage the passage of anti-traditional family measures. For example, recent research regarding brain development in infants and its relation to the constant interaction, stimulation, and attention of the baby's caregiver was emphasized at a recent White

House conference. Supporters of the new child care measures used this research to argue not for the need for more maternal interaction with children but for the need to improve the quality of federally subsidized commercial care by increasing its budget.[23] Similarly, advocates of increased federal spending on child care point to the projected increases in the percentages of working mothers and single-parent families as a prima facie argument that the demand for out-of-home child care services will increase by a proportional amount, and that these working mothers must be assured of "affordable, quality care." Of course, this ignores the actual care choices that working mothers are making for their children: of the approximately ten million children whose moms are employed, half are cared for by fathers, grandmothers, and other family members in the home. The logical way of allowing working mothers to choose among different options of child care would be to provide all mothers of pre-schoolers with a per-child tax credit that could be used for commercial care, at-home care, or even to allow the mother to forgo work and raise her own children if she so wishes. But that option, of course, cannot be conceded by the professional child care lobby.

Instead, the Clinton proposal is a combination of new subsidies for states promoting commercial care, tax credits for businesses that open or expand child care centers, expanded tax credits for individuals who use commercial day care, and scholarships for child care workers. This hardly reflects a neutral agenda with regard to enabling mothers to make a choice between at-home and commercial care. Clearly, the first aim of the child care activists—just as for the original proponents of government subsidies for commercial child care—is to keep mothers on the career track at all costs.

Since stating their true aim so candidly would not be acceptable to the public at large, child care activists point to the economic costs that would result from mothers leaving the workforce to raise their children. At the recent White House conference on child care, Treasury Secretary Robert Rubin argued that federally-subsidized child care is a necessity if the U.S. is to remain competitive in the global economy: "My great concern is that this prosperity will mask the challenges that we face. A key question is: how do we create an environment that will increase productivity? The answer is that we need a flexible and mobile workforce to which everyone can contribute to the limits of their ability."[24] Rubin's "great concern" about maintaining competitiveness echoes those business leaders of the late 1950s who regarded the participation of married mothers in the workforce as essential for continued economic expansion. The treasury secretary praised several corporations for getting 94 percent of new mothers to return to work after having a child.

But revealingly, Rubin acknowledged that the forces of the free market alone, without federal assistance, are insufficient to meet the child care needs of the large number of working mothers. We need a "private-public partnership" and a "massive effort to improve citizen knowledge about what we need to do to succeed in the global economy."[25] In other words, without more federal subsidies for day care, mothers will leave the workforce and U.S. businesses will be put at a competitive disadvantage in the world market.

Because the cost of maintaining this competitiveness is very expensive for families—an estimated twelve thousand dollars a year for adequate infant day care—many of those families would, no doubt, determine that the advantages of a second income are merely illusory once the cost of nonparental care is taken into account. Without subsidies, it simply makes no financial sense for most families to get someone else to raise their kids. Perhaps this should come as no surprise; as far back as 1920, G. K. Chesterton pointed out the absurdity of this arrangement to child care advocates of his own day: "If people cannot mind their own business, it cannot possibly be more economical to pay them to mind each other's business, and still less to mind each other's babies. . . . Ultimately, we are arguing that a woman should not be a mother to her own baby, but a nursemaid to somebody else's baby. But it will not work, even on paper."[26]

So the "child care crisis" boils down to the fact that it simply makes no economic or rational sense for mothers to work in order to pay strangers to raise their children, just as the "feminization of poverty" boils down to the fact that working mothers who are single parents have discovered that they are unable to pursue their career, raise their children, and maintain a reasonable standard of living without the income of a husband. The professional child care lobby, however, seems impervious to the commonsense notion that the normal, and preferable, arrangement for most people is to take care of their own children. Hence Patty Siegel, a child care consultant in California, can say indignantly and without apparent irony: "The child care crisis is so acute that child care workers in many areas of the country are unable to find adequate day care for their own children."[27]

Such rhetoric, however, has convinced elite opinion, (including the political class in Washington) that the child care crisis is not a crisis of parental care, but of commercial care. Even the GOP-controlled Senate—theoretically less amenable to the concept of "socialized" child rearing than the Clinton Administration—overwhelmingly approved a measure granting tax credits for businesses that set up child care facilities for their employees. The child care debate illustrates well that family issues in the future will not break down along typical liberal pro-government vs. conservative anti-government lines; the divide, rather, is between those who believe parental care of children is of vital importance and those who do not. The same division is perceptible on a host of other issues, including the latest battlefront, proposals for year-round school and all-day kindergarten for children. Behind these proposed measures we find the same alliance of careerist mothers and business interests worried about global competitiveness. The rhetoric is about accelerating the learning curve and improving academic performance, but the impetus behind the year-round schooling movement is that dual-income families find such an arrangement convenient. Opponents are generally parents who want to spend more time with their children.

The politics of the next decade will, to a great extent, revolve around the issue of whether parental care of children within the context of the traditional two-parent family is, or is not, an indispensable social norm. On one side of the issue are those who want to subvert that norm for the sake of women's careers or for the sake of business productivity and global competitiveness. On the other side are those who believe that there is no adequate substitute for parental care, and that all attempts to alleviate the crisis in child care by other means will only contribute to the breakup of the family and the breakdown of society.

Those who contend that the family is an infinitely malleable institution, and that the arrangement of domestic life—including the upbringing of children—is a mere matter of social custom have much against them to contend with in the way of historical example. It is not only in post-1960s America that the radical experiment of dispensing with traditional forms of family life and child care has led to economic dislocation and social chaos; other societies in the twentieth century have traveled the same path deliberately. In the decade after the bolsheviks took power in Soviet Russia, the new Soviet government instituted "family codes" providing for the "collectivized upbringing of children" and changed legal definitions of what constituted a family, which facilitated easy divorce, abolished distinctions between legitimate and illegitimate birth, and gave women greater economic rights in marriage. The new laws led to such rapid family disintegration and social chaos that they were completely abandoned by the mid-1930s. By the next decade, Soviet leaders had even reinstated the old inheritance laws in order to provide families more reason to stay together.

Like the Soviet reformers, the American family law reformers of the 1960s are now reaping the economic and social consequences of their revolution. But unlike the old bolsheviks they show no sign of turning back. The revolution in divorce law and in the culture of marriage are perhaps the best example of their intransigence. Feminist thinkers and activists in the women's movement in the late 1960s and early 1970s assured women that the enactment of no-fault divorce laws would mean their liberation from bad marriages and their economic independence. No-fault laws were passed by nearly every state in the nation soon after 1970, largely at the instigation of feminist organizations. Although there is some dispute about their precise effect on the divorce rate due to the timing of the implementation of no-fault theory, there is now little doubt that they accelerated the cultural trend towards divorce, which only peaked in the early 1980s and has stayed at record levels ever since. What is beyond question is that no-fault has made divorce considerably easier to obtain for the spouse that wants out of a marriage, without regard for the wishes of the other spouse. It essentially transferred the right to decide when divorce is justified from society to the individual, leaving the marriage contract gutted and legally meaningless. After the institution of no-fault divorce laws, says Maggie Gallagher, marriage has turned into "something best described as cohabitation with insurance benefits."[28]

Moreover, making marriages subject to unilateral dissolution resulted in none of the economic benefits to women predicted by its feminist advocates. On the contrary, numerous studies have shown that divorce usually impoverishes women and children while enriching men.[29] From 1970 to 1983, just as the divorce rate was going through the roof, so was the number of children living in poverty; 65 percent of that increase occurred in the fast-growing number of female-headed families.[30] And because "women's advocates" have effectively demolished all remaining protections for women in the law on the theory that the principle of "equal treatment" is essential for women's advancement, courts are less likely to award custody of children to the wife in a divorce proceeding, which makes women more likely to agree to a reduced settlement in order to retain custody.[31]

As the economic damage that divorce inflicts on women has become more apparent, feminists have stressed that women need divorce-on-demand so that battered wives can escape abusive husbands.

The correlation of domestic violence and marriage is simply asserted. In fact, spousal abuse accounts for just 9 percent of all domestic violence. A full two-thirds of male abusers are either boyfriends or ex-husbands. Such data should lead us to strengthen the bonds of marriage, not to weaken them. Of course, the argument that legal obstacles to divorce might result in a wife's being forced to remain in an abusive marriage is used primarily for its emotional impact. In reality, divorce for reasons of abusive conduct on the part of a spouse was easily obtainable—and was commonly granted—long before the advent of no-fault laws.[32]

From child care to marriage law, the common thread running through the policy prescriptions of the new feminists and their allies in the business world—no matter what the rhetoric has emphasized—has been the transfer of women's loyalties from family to career. This has entailed weakening the bonds of the traditional family, particularly those that provide the economic and legal security necessary for married mothers to raise children in the home. It has also meant constructing a system of incentives to encourage and reward the workforce participation of married mothers and to make the choice of nonparental child care more feasible. Of course, the corollary to this new order is that the same system punishes those families who wish to live by more traditional domestic arrangements and particularly those married mothers who wish to care for their own children.

Preserving the Family

Those inclined to defend the family from these mortal threats to its security and well-being in the realms of public policy and economy have been at a loss as to how to proceed. This is largely because they have, consciously or unconsciously, accepted many of the premises of radical individualism that underlie the philosophy of their opponents—particularly the notion that empowering individual choice in a free society requires the weakening of the power of assumed com-

mitments, such as marriage and children, commitments that are at the
core of family life and domestic existence. They must begin to question those premises, for when society assists some individuals to
evade the responsibilities of their freely assumed commitments (in
the name of "choice"), the security and, indeed, the freedom of those
who abide by the commitments they have made are diminished.

Those concerned about family decline must simply and forthrightly acknowledge that the traditional family structure in which the
mother is the principal caregiver to her children is a necessary institution, indeed a prerequisite, for the maintenance of the social order
and the very continuation of society, and that it follows that all public-policy decisions must be measured by how they affect the family.
This is far from being a reactionary notion propounded only by "social conservatives": the idea was first put forth by liberal Senator
Walter Mondale in the 1970s in the form of the Family Impact Statement, which proposed that every major new policy, before being enacted, must be assessed for its impact on the family.[33] The World
Congress of Families put forth a similar proposal in 1997 in Prague,
which included a rather orthodox definition of the family:

> The family is a man and a woman in a lifelong covenant of marriage for the purposes of:
> - the continuation of the human species
> - the rearing of children
> - the regulation of sexuality
> - the provision of mutual support and protection
> - the creation of an altruistic home economy, and
> - the maintenance of bonds between the generations.
>
> Every existing and proposed public policy *should be measured*
> by lawmakers against these questions:
>
> Will this policy strengthen or weaken these natural family
> functions?
>
> Will this policy increase or diminish family autonomy?[34]

While it is unquestionable that the United States has a long and entrenched tradition of individual freedom, it is also true that part of that tradition—a part that Americans have always understood intuitively—was that individual freedom cannot be preserved without the mediating institution of the family. Without the protection of the family, individual freedom is at the mercy of the commercial forces of the market, the intellectual and cultural manipulation of the mass media, and perhaps most menacingly, the tyranny of government. It is no accident that the philosophy of radical individualism and the socialist tendency toward big, bureaucratic government have always gone hand in hand; when the vital intermediate institution of the family does not protect the freedom of its individual members within the context of domestic life, government will inevitably step in as the final guarantor of *absolute* individual liberty from everything that might constrain it, including the family itself. Of course, this absolute freedom turns out to be illusory as the individual finds the sphere of his freedom is diminished to the point of insignificance outside of its natural domestic domain, and the government is obliged to perform family functions when that natural system of mutual support and sustenance that is the family breaks down.

Several major principles of reform aimed at strengthening families—all based on the reality that maintaining traditional families is a social and economic necessity—present themselves:

1) *Treat families as a unit in the tax code.* Restoring "income splitting," for example, would end the marriage penalty, creating a financial incentive to marry and a disincentive to divorce.

2) *End "no-fault" divorce.* With unilateral divorce on demand, the spouse who takes primary responsibility for child care and homemaking—almost always the wife—has virtually no economic security, because they have no enforceable legal claim

on the income of the breadwinner. Moving in the direction of a system of optional "covenant" marriage—such as has been enacted in the state of Louisiana—would send a much-needed message to homemakers and mothers that society values their work highly and will not tolerate their abandonment.

3) *Replace the current welfare system with an anti-poverty policy that does not encourage illegitimacy at the expense of intact families.* Benefits and tax exemptions should never be higher for children born out of wedlock than for those born to a married couple, and all benefits to unmarried mothers should be contingent on identification of the father.

4) *Delete the word "sex" from Title VII of the Civil Rights Act of 1964.* So long as there is an equating in employment law of racial minorities and women, employers will continue to be prevented from making pay distinctions between those with family responsibilities and those without, and the bogus principle of "proportional representation" (which holds that if women represent anything less than 50 percent of the workforce in any given profession, this represents "discrimination") will be perpetuated. Such a principle fails to acknowledge the choice of women to take care of their children and families at home—or it makes that choice invalid.

5) *Do not discriminate against single-income married couples or housewives in the tax code.* Instead of allowing special tax breaks for the use of commercial child care, give all married couples equal treatment, allowing deductions or credits per child to enable families to decide for themselves what type of care they prefer. In addition, allow homemakers to contribute to Individual Retirement Accounts. Currently, dual-income couples are allowed to put away four thousand dollars

annually in IRAS; single-income families only $2,250 a year. Allowing homemakers to contribute equally up to two thousand dollars would remedy this inequity.

6) *Protect families from government and business invasion into the "domestic economy."* One of the primary responsibilities and rights of parents is the education and upbringing of their children; government's regulatory reach into the home—both with regard to home education of children and child neglect accusations—should be strictly limited by law. In addition, outdated zoning laws that prevent work in the home—most passed at the instigation of big business interests who saw domestic labor as a threat to industrialization of the economy—should be eliminated to allow more home-work options.[35]

All truly "family-friendly" policy reforms must be based on the conscious social reinforcement of the married couple with children raised at home. This understanding of the family as the basic unit of society is an ancient legal and intellectual tradition in Western world, perhaps first elaborated by Aristotle in his *Politics,* where he explained that the family household is the basic unit of society because it is the smallest unit capable of reproducing and sustaining itself. As Mary Ann Glendon has noted, European nations tend to have more explicit recognition of marriage and family in their legal and constitutional systems than does the United States; which is why, for instance, they have not gone so far as to institute "no-fault" divorce.[36] But perhaps an even more significant barrier than the legal tradition to truly family-friendly policy reforms in the U.S. is a reigning economic theory that does not acknowledge the family and its essential role in producing what is by far the most important aspect of the economy: human capital.

The notion of "human capital" is an economic theory devised to account for the burst of economic growth in the post-World War II period that was not predicted by the then-dominant neo-classical school of economists. The assumption up until that time had always been that all growth comes from investment in "nonhuman" capital, such as machines and buildings. In the past two decades, many economists have accounted for the significant "missing growth" by positing that "earnings unrelated to investment in human capital [such as education, training, informal learning and child rearing in general] are a small part of the total," according to leading proponent Gary Becker.[37]

While the theory of human capital has limitations (it tends to measure the worth of all human activity in terms of market utility, and thus can be an intrusion of the business mentality into the domestic sphere), it is useful for quantifying the vital contribution that investment in people makes to the "productive" market economy. For the vast majority of families, wages are the most important part of income; and investment in child rearing and education (which determine future employment possibilities and compensation) are the most important form of saving. Economist John Mueller has estimated that two-thirds of gross national income is labor compensation earned from earlier investment in "human capital," noting that this proportion has remained constant for over a century, with workers contributing about two-thirds, and property-owners about one-third, to increases in total output. But because the tax code treats this investment in human capital as "consumption" rather than "savings," three-quarters of all federal taxes are levied on personal income. [38]

What economist Theodore Schultz said in 1960 is still true today: "Our tax laws everywhere discriminate against human capital" and work "in favor of nonhuman capital."[39] In fact since World War II the tax on property income has actually declined, while the tax on labor has risen and continues to rise.[40]

In practical terms, this means that the hundreds of thousands of dollars that a family spends on food, clothing, and education for children is all considered "consumption" and taxed, while that same money put into a building or a piece of machinery is considered investment, and can be written off. Current standard deductions and exemptions do not even begin to cover the minimal "maintenance cost" of keeping children alive, much less investments in their health, education, or skills. And all of the tax reform proposals now on the table, even those that advertise themselves as pro-family, only worsen this disparity, increasing deductions for machines and buildings, and disallowing similar write-offs for investment in human capital. Many of the proposals being considered would even eliminate currently allowed deductions or credits for "human maintenance," meaning the share of the tax burden levied on human capital would rise from three-fourths to close to 100 percent.[41]

All truly pro-family tax reforms would move in precisely the opposite direction, on the principle that human capital should be treated no worse than nonhuman capital. Economist Mueller suggests that this could be achieved by allowing deductions only for the cost of maintaining both human and nonhuman capital: hence all wages below the poverty level (representing a minimum standard of human maintenance) would be exempt from taxation, while all deductions currently allowed for acquiring nonhuman capital ("expensing" or "depreciating") would be eliminated, with all capital taxed at a low marginal rate of around 17 percent.[42] Others have proposed combining a modest increase in the personal exemption (perhaps to four thousand dollars) with a significantly increased, fifteen-hundred-dollar tax credit for every child in the United States. This could lighten substantially the tax burden of families with children and could replace the destructive system of welfare payments.

Another proposal, also based on the recognition of the economic value of human capital, seems less wise, because it attempts to place a market value on all human activity. Economist Gary Becker has proposed that the nonmarket time of students and parents should be "expensed" for tax purposes, on the theory that time spent on any valuable nonmarket activity can be calculated in terms of forgone

wages or "opportunity cost," and hence compensated.[43] The fundamental problem with this idea is that it attempts a concrete valuation
of invaluable things, such as care and love for one's children, leisure,
worship, and the other intangibles of domestic life that by definition
can have no price affixed to them. It also opens the door for the taxation of this nonmarket time if the cost can be precisely calculated.

While policy changes aimed at making the economy and the tax
code more friendly to families are important, they are not enough.
Just as policy changes that worked against the family cannot entirely
explain the family decline that began after the end of the baby boom
in the mid-1960s, policy changes favorable to family formation and
unity will not entirely remedy the situation. There has always been
and will continue to be a large cultural element in private decisions
regarding the family, an element that includes confidence in the future, religious belief and practice, and the cultural status accorded
nonmarket work. If the cultural status of the housewife is not sufficient to compete against the consumerist attractions of disposable income, no number of policy reforms will be sufficient to reinforce the
decision of a mother to devote herself to children and family.

Policy reforms can make the economy and the legal system more
amenable to the traditional single-income family with children. But
what can be done to make the culture more amenable?

∾ 6 ∾

Striking a Balance

*Whereas the American mother is the greatest source of the
country's strength and inspiration . . . Whereas the American mother is doing so much for the home, for moral
spirits and religion, hence so much for good government
and humanity . . . Therefore, be it resolved that the second
Sunday in May will be celebrated as Mother's Day.*

U.S. Congressional resolution, 1914

*Who is Mom? Everything today, and more than she was
given credit for yesterday. . . . Mothers can be married,
single, divorced, step, surrogate, foster, adoptive, gay,
straight, or 63 years old.*

Boston Globe editorial, Mother's Day 1997

AN ECONOMIC ENVIRONMENT AND A BUSINESS ETHIC that favors the
formation and maintenance of traditional families are much needed,
but even more crucial is recognition by our culture that mothers who

devote themselves to raising their own children at home are performing a vital task. Decisions about child care, ideas about work and leisure, even aspirations for the future—all of these are formed in response to subtle and not-so-subtle messages of cultural acceptability received from schools, popular press, literature, and entertainment. If young mothers who go back to work as soon as possible after giving birth are cultural heroes—if those who put their children and families second to professional attainment are singled out as models—we should not be surprised that fewer women are devoting themselves to children and family, even if such devotion is necessary.

Consider the publicity given Take Our Daughters to Work Day. The ostensible purpose of Take Our Daughters to Work Day, started by Gloria Steinem's Ms. Foundation in 1993, is to expose young girls to role models of professional women, the assumption being that this is necessary for them to overcome any remnant of social stereotyping that prevents them from achieving in the workforce.[1] When one contrasts the news media coverage of Mother's Day with that of Take Our Daughters to Work Day, one finds not simply public recognition of admirable women, but unabashed cultural propaganda.

As often as not, Mother's Day is treated as an editorial opportunity to debunk the supposed maternalist myths on which America is founded. In the *Baltimore Sun* Julia Vitullo-Martin informed us on Mother's Day 1998 that

> The original Mother's Day, like all our best holidays, is of Pagan origin. It was a celebration in Asia Minor in honor of Cybele. . . . A form of Mother's Day returned, this time in honor of the church. In the fifth century, devotion to the Virgin Mary emerged as a new mother cult, with this mother of God firmly replacing Cybele, the mother of the gods. Meanwhile, in the Celtic continent and British Isles, the powerful goddess Brigit was replaced by St. Brigid, her Christian successor. Her sacred Mother's Day, which was connected with the ewes coming into milk, became St. Brigid's Day. . . . While celebrating Mother's Day

as the romantic, commercial holiday that it has become, we should ponder the triumph and ferocity of motherhood that lies beneath its sweet surface.[2]

Whereas the *Sun* saw fit to serve as a mouthpiece for contentious feminist "herstory" on Mother's Day, the *Los Angeles Times* used the occasion not to honor mothers but to congratulate "mothers who aren't": "Sure, bring on the flowers, candy and cards today. But as we honor mothers, kudos also are in order for a big crop of mothers who aren't. Not yet anyway. . . . The consequences of teen parenthood touch the mother, her child and all of us. For teenage girls, motherhood means that dreams of completing their education or launching a career are often deferred or dashed."[3]

The press indulges in cynical "maternal myth" debunking on Mother's Day, but on Take Our Daughters to Work Day the reporting is positively solemn in its homage to working moms. The *Washington Post* breathlessly related that young girls

> followed a Cabinet member to Capitol Hill and the White House, watched workers paint cars in a Silver Spring auto body shop, learned about Chicago's mercantile exchange by trading pizza and brainstormed on how to design a car in Detroit. . . . At a Capitol Hill breakfast held by the Women's Campaign Fund, three girls from Amidon School in southwest Washington had juice and rolls with Deputy Education Secretary Madeleine M. Kunin and announced their own career goals: neurosurgeon, pediatrician, corporate lawyer. It was just what the organizers of this event wanted to hear.
>
> "It's marvelous that they have this grand vision," said Kunin, who spent the day with one of the girls. "Our charge is to make sure that vision doesn't get abbreviated, doesn't get a shadow cast over it."[4]

Columnist Katha Pollitt wrote in the *Chicago Tribune* that while she likes Take Our Daughters to Work Day, she is afraid it does not go far enough:

> Wouldn't it be better to take them to . . . a demonstration? In
> Germany this March, thousands of women took to the street to
> kick off Women's Action Week. On International Women's Day,
> tens of thousands went on strike. . . . German Parliament Presi-
> dent Rita Suessmuth called for hiring preferences for homemak-
> ers returning to the job and a quota system to ensure job equality
> for women. Why can't we do something like that here?
>
> Think of it: streams of women and girls pouring from work-
> places and schools out into the streets with a list of serious de-
> mands—equal pay, comparable worth, affordable day care,
> nonsexist schooling with realistic sex education, free contracep-
> tion and abortion on demand, paid parental leave and gender
> parity in both houses of Congress.

While such a vision probably did not strike most of Pollitt's readers
as all that enticing, the point of the coverage of Take Our Daughters
to Work Day was clear: to confer cultural status on women at work
to the detriment of women at home.[5]

If it is true, as I am contending, that cultural respectability is as
important to individual family choices as economic or social climate,
then the postwar Baby Boom must have cultural explanations as well
as the policy explanations already explored. The period from 1946
to 1964 was an anomaly and was followed by a sharp decline in family vitality that continues up to our own day. Scholars have long
puzzled over this. The Baby Boom was a period during which single-
income, mother-at-home families showed renewed signs of vitality in
nearly every statistical measurement, including higher fertility rates,
lower divorce rates, and declining labor force participation of women
of childbearing age. We have already discussed the changes in economic and tax policy, and some students of the era do discern a combination of cultural elements that contributed to this domestic
renaissance.

Harvard's Richard Gill has suggested that the apparent family vitality of this era was a result of postwar American optimism and

confidence in future prospects. This optimism, which Gill terms the belief in the "Idea of Progress," had the effect of renewing the impulse to sacrifice immediate satisfactions for the sake of one's children. "The only possible explanation for these phenomenal, and wholly unexpected, changes," writes Gill, "would be a sudden, unequivocal reinvigoration of the Idea of Progress in the two decades following the end of World War ii. . . . The end of the war was succeeded by a strong revival of faith in the future. Did any of those postwar parents of the Baby Boom have even a moment's doubt that their children would lead better and happier lives than they had? Not very likely. Their faith in their children's futures was as strong, and in some respects even more intense, than that of their Victorian forebears half a century before." A dramatic increase in relative income, the relative tranquility of American society at home and abroad, and the confident cultural dominance of the "affluent society" ideal around the world all combined, in Gill's view, to produce a period of unusual vitality for the traditional family in the United States.

So what accounts for the relatively sudden collapse of optimism and the reversal of the positive family trends that followed immediately on this period? Gill contends that the difference between the postwar optimism about the future and comparable periods of American family vitality (such as the progressive era at the turn of the century) is that the belief in the "Idea of Progress" that characterized earlier ages had always been accompanied by the conviction that inculcating discipline in the next generation was the price of continued progress: "There was a major missing ingredient [in the Baby Boom parents' Idea of Progress]. And this missing ingredient was the morality embodied in the Idea of Progress, or perhaps even more narrowly, the discipline embodied therein. . . . What was different was that they seemed to see no reason that their children should not sit back and indulge themselves in the better life that was now available." This indulgent attitude towards children, combined with the social and cultural convulsions of the 1960s, led to the more self-centered, present-oriented behavior of the Baby Boom generation. Lacking an inherited ethic of hard work and self-discipline, disillusioned about their own and America's prospects, pessimistic regarding the future of mankind itself in light of contemporary predictions of resource shortages, overpopulation, and environmental catastrophe, the Baby Boom generation proceeded to "live for today," while families—based as they are on self-sacrifice, discipline, and deferred gratification— proceeded to fall apart.

The economic attractions and cultural incentives that push married mothers into the paid workforce are so strong today, suggests Gill, that if society really determines that parental care is essential for children (particularly young children), then it will have to make up for the "opportunity cost" incurred by parents who sacrifice earnings and career advancement potential during the years they spend raising their preschool children. Since Gill himself believes that "it should be considered a responsibility of parents to provide primary care for their children until they are of school age except in the most unusual circumstances," he proposes what he calls a "parental bill of rights," the most important provision of which would provide "mothers, or fathers as the case may be" with "a subsidy in return for the career sacrifice they are making for a socially desirable end." In most cases, he allows, that early nurturing and caregiving will take place "primarily with the mothers," and "paternal exceptions" would be "rare." While noting that "the percentage of a woman's life during which she will have a child of five or under in the house has declined precipitously since the last century, probably now to 10 percent or even less," he maintains that "mothers who forgo labor force participation during their child-rearing years do have to pay a substantial price for having done so," citing estimates that a woman returning to the workforce after child rearing earns a wage "33 percent lower than it otherwise would have been and that most of them never fully make up this difference later in life." Providing these mothers with subsidies for supplemental education, job training, and lost wages to make up for their interrupted career is the course he recommends.[6]

Although much of Gill's analysis of the cultural reasons for the domestic renaissance has merit, his picture of the cultural currents that contributed to the reversal of family fortunes that characterized the 1950s remains inadequate and incomplete. In the first place, it does not account for the religious element of the family vitality of the postwar era. When one breaks down the statistics according to religious practice, it becomes apparent that the Baby Boom was largely a Catholic phenomenon that took place in a time of unusual cultural unity among American Catholics, during which the hierarchy unabashedly promoted the virtues of large traditional families. As I suggested earlier, the surprisingly strong cultural resonance of the notions of home as domestic prison and career as self-fulfillment depended in large measure on preexisting cultural conceptions of work and home. The idea that work outside the home is a glamorous opportunity for power and increased cultural status—over against the menial tasks that homemaking and child-rearing comprise—did not originate with the new feminists of the early 1960s. As Gill's analysis implies, the cultural devaluation of the housewife and mother went along with the postwar version of the American Dream that emphasized material prosperity—rather than internal family harmony and a vital domestic existence—as the measure of the good life. But what Gill proposes—direct subsidies for mothers to make up for lost earnings opportunities—would only accentuate the problem by reinforcing the view that the only work our society truly values is market-related, and that even child-rearing can be measured in terms of its market value and social utility. As economist John Mueller has written, the market value of domestic time—be it time devoted to raising children or simply leisure—"of its nature, cannot even in theory be measured or even estimated. Time spent praying, or dancing, or reading poetry, or hearing Mozart, or witnessing Shakespeare, or even in strenuous child-rearing, is not prayer or poetry or music or Shakespeare or child-rearing at all, if an economic taxi-meter is always running in the background, ticking off a supposed price measured as the cost in forgone earnings."[7] Gill's solution would, in fact, encourage the further devaluation of the mother and housewife by implying that no married mother in her right mind would want to sacrifice valuable time from a promising career merely for her family, without a guarantee that society would help her to get back on the career track as soon as possible after the unpleasant interlude.

Changing the Culture

If our culture so undervalues hearth and home and the work done there, then there may be no choice but to change the culture. Toward that end, an effort must be made to restore cultural status to the mother and homemaker, not just for the social utility of those roles but for their intrinsic value. At the same time, we must debunk the myth that work outside the home is the best opportunity our culture offers for self-fulfillment and self-expression.

There are several small, encouraging indications that this myth is beginning to lose its force. For one thing, there has been a statistical leveling-off of the workforce participation rates of married mothers with young children in the past several years: in 1997, the rate declined for the first time since the 1950s.[8] This could be a result of personal experience with the inadequacy of alternatives to parental care of young children. It could even be an indication that evidence of the detrimental effects of commercial child care on young children is beginning to have and effect, despite the lack of attention given to the accumulating data on this subject by the media and the medical community. It may also signal that personal experience confirms the inadequacy of the corporate setting as a place of self-affirmation and personal fulfillment.

Today, the most compelling arguments for staying at home to raise the children are coming not from women who have always been stay-at-home mothers, but from women who are professionally experienced and accomplished and who have discovered, to their surprise, the joys of mothering. Economist Jennifer Roback Morse wrote recently about her conversion from the view that some women have careers that are too important to sacrifice in order to take care of their own children: "These are things I might have said in the days before I became a mother, when I could analyze child care as nothing but an economic issue. But when I consider my own particular children, rather than hypothetical children, I cannot be convinced for a minute of the truth of these claims. There is no good substitute for my care. I can hire help once in awhile, but hired help cannot create a home or raise a child."[9]

The visceral reaction against entrusting the upbringing of one's own children to a third party, when actually faced with the decision, is a common theme with mothers who have jumped off the career track. Diane Wormsbaker, formerly an executive assistant at Ameristar Corporation, alludes to the same phenomenon in her own case: "Going to work was such a big part of my life that it was hard to imagine not doing it. But after my first daughter was born, I knew I couldn't be the mother that I wanted to be if I stayed on the job." Having decided to be a full-time mom, she had to overcome the fear of economic insecurity resulting from the loss of a second income. "I had to prove to myself—and to my husband, who was skeptical about the loss of income—that we could do it." Her solution was simply to scale back. "You find ways to save money. You're not working, so you don't eat out as much. And you can buy food in bigger quantities and cook, and that saves money. . . . I think it comes down to being willing to live with less."[10] But Catherine Carbone Rogers, a former television reporter who is now the publicity director for an organization of nonworking mothers, notes that the economic and social sacrifices entailed in the decision to forgo professional work are far from easy: "Obviously, quitting is a step that not every working mother can afford to take, and it's not something you should do without some soul-searching. What happens to your 401(k)? What about health insurance? When you're ready to go back to the workforce, will there be jobs that you're interested in doing?" In a society without the economic and cultural supports that facilitate the decision to take time out to raise one's own children, notes Carbone Rogers, feelings of isolation and abandonment can be a serious matter. "In the '50s and '60s, you could find a neighborhood full of mothers at home. Now, if you stay home, you're often the only one in your neighborhood who's doing it."[11]

Not only do they constitute a distinct minority of their peers, but full-time moms also face the undermining of their choice by the cultural message that only inferior women would choose to stay at home. Roback Morse frankly acknowledges that the aversion to the notion of home and motherhood that was typical of her post-1960s generation of mothers was not innate and unprogrammed. Most of the negative feelings about domestic life were the result of cultural conditioning that came before these women had much real-life experience: "Some of us have come to believe that our self-esteem depends upon our jobs, or that we appear weak if we admit that taking care of children is enjoyable. Some women assume that child care is mind-numbing, spirit-killing drudgery, and that only work outside the home is fulfilling. These are not necessarily statements that women would come up with spontaneously, in the absence of feminist tutoring." She says that the dogma that one's earning capacity equals one's influence in society is essentially materialistic and is a view of the world unworthy of any parent, but particularly unworthy of mothers: "[D]ollar power is not the only kind of power. Losing control over what happens to one's children is for many women a devastating loss of power. Surrendering day-to-day contact with one's children, giving up the ability to influence their development, surely these count as losses of power for any mother or father."[12]

Just as the caricature of childrearing and homemaking as "mind-numbing, spirit-killing drudgery" bears little relation to the reality of domestic life as actually lived, Morse is acute about where true power and true job satisfaction are to be found: "Instead of introducing their own children to great literature and world history, bright women are sequestered in university offices, grading piles of illegible midterms written by other people's children. How did we forget that guiding our offspring requires knowledge far more subtle, and pays bounties far richer, than most jobs?"[13]

Morse argues that—despite the attractions and perks of the modern workplace—the reality that the majority of working mothers find there is far from the romantic picture painted by feminist advocates of "having it all": "It is attachment to their wives and children that keeps men reporting as truck mechanics and cab drivers. It is a sense of loving duty that keeps men standing on subway platforms that lead to fluorescent-lit offices. The drudgery of caring for small children is nothing compared to the drudgery of factory work or a data entry job. For many workers, the tedium of a humdrum job is relieved more than anything else by coming home to a noisy household."[14]

In her own case, Morse discovered that domesticity entailed far more challenges, both intellectual and professional, than her career in academia: "It took me an embarrassingly long time to realize that my two children needed me at home more than they needed anything my income would buy for them. It took even longer for me to realize that placing my intellect at the service of my family was a greater challenge than my ordinary life as a university professor. I had accepted far more feminist premises than I had realized."[15]

Journalist Iris Krasnow discovered that all the feminist rhetoric of emancipation through work was only actually fulfilled when she "surrendered" to motherhood. "Choosing to be a mother who spends most of her time with her sons is actually a convergence of the feminist ideals my era of women embraced—power, freedom self-expression, and independence. Nothing ever felt so powerful, so free, so spiritually right, as becoming a militant mother who organizes a home and fights for her children on every front." For Krasnow, this revelation came only through personal experience. After having consciously rejected being a housewife like her mother in favor of a "glamorous" career interviewing celebrities for United Press International, she now has different feelings about stay-at-home motherhood: "When I was a college student at Stanford in the 1970s, the sight of my own stay-at-home mother wearing her red-checked dish towel slung over one shoulder used to rile me as a symbol of the oppression of wives stuck in their kitchens. . . . Then came marriage, the birth of four sons in rapid succession, and a departure from daily journalism to raise children and become a free-lance writer at home. Ironically, when I now wear a red-checked dish towel over my shoulder as my mother did, I don't feel oppressed; I feel happy and free."

Krasnow also came to the conclusion that the strict dichotomy between work and home perpetuated by the popular culture was utterly false: "Being a good journalist requires intense energy and devotion; being a good mother takes at least the same commitment, if not more. To succeed, I knew that I would have to work harder than I'd ever worked on anything in my life."[16]

Even mothers who have achieved the highest levels of professional prestige and accomplishment commonly voice regrets about having let the most important years of their children's development slip by without sufficient attention. Zelda Fichandler, founder of the Arena Stage in Washington, D.C., was asked in an interview if she had any regrets. "If I had a perfect life to live over again," she answered, "I would spend the first five years of my children's lives at home. At the time, I never felt guilty about leaving the kids. I kept feeling 'this is worth it.' Now I give advice to young women to be very careful whether it's worth it. I'm not absolutely positive now that it's been worth it. . . . I never had enough of my kids."[17] The former Israeli Prime Minister, the late Golda Meir, told an interviewer of the conflict that exists between motherhood and career, no matter how important that career may be: "Such a struggle breaks out in you. Your heart goes to pieces. It's all running around, trying to be in two places at once, getting upset. All this can't help but be reflected in the structure of the family. I know that my children, when they were little, suffered a lot on my account. I left them alone so often. I was never with them when I should have been and would have liked to be. . . . If you only knew how many times I say to myself, 'To hell with everything, to hell with everybody, I've done my share, now let the others do theirs, enough, enough, enough.'"[18]

Several organizations have sprung up in recent years composed of former career women who are now full-time mothers. One such group is FEMALE (Formerly Employed Mothers at the Leading Edge), with 142 local chapters in thirty states. Ninety-six percent of FEMALE's members intend to return to work when their children are older. According to Richard Hokenson, chief economist for the brokerage firm Donaldson, Lufkin & Jenrette, groups such as FEMALE may indeed be at the "leading edge" of a new demographic trend towards mothers interrupting their careers for significant periods to stay at home with their children. While two-income couples still outnumber one-earner families by two to one, Hokenson believes that the long-term trend of mothers of young children to work "is now in the process of reversing," citing a slight narrowing of the gap in the past few years.[19] In Hokenson's analysis, some families have used the savings resulting from lower mortgage rates in the past few years to allow one earner—usually the wife—to work part-time or leave a job altogether. Others cite recent congressional passage of a four hundred dollar-per-child tax credit as the occasion for more families inclined towards maternal care of the children to put their beliefs into action. Some critics, such as feminist historian Stephanie Coontz, dismiss the significance of these statistics as "a trendlet, a mini-trend among the affluent, just in the last few years. It's a status symbol now, a class thing."[20]

Nevertheless, there is some indication that the decision to forgo career for the sake of family is becoming marginally more acceptable in the culture. When, on the birth of her child, Brenda Barnes resigned her job as president and CEO of Pepsi-Cola North America, the reaction of op-ed writers across the country was more sympathetic than one might have expected, although feminist writers predictably regarded her decision as a betrayal of working women.[21]

The literature of another group dedicated to supporting women in their decision to leave paid work for the sake of their children, Mothers At Home, eloquently expresses both the cultural pressures faced by young mothers today and the newfound confidence of some to be "countercultural":

> By the time we headed for college or set out to "make it on our own," a simple but trenchant message spoke from the pages of virtually every book, newspaper, and magazine: "Smart women go to work." Indeed, it seemed treasonous not to, especially in the presence of those who had fought the battles before us, ostensibly on our behalf.
>
> So completely were we surrounded by infallible models of the modern woman that it never occurred to us that we weren't the only ones having a hard time making it all work. . . .
>
> [Some mothers today] want to be home because in some quiet moment caring for their children, they have suddenly experienced the vastness, the intricacies, the delicate nature of this work. While performing some entirely routine act of nurturing, they have unexpectedly stumbled on a moment of insight so luminous as to reveal with imposing clarity that the greatest opportunity for success they might ever have is nestled right there in their arms.

Janet Dittmer, co-author of *What's a Smart Woman Like You Doing at Home?*, confirms that notions of what constitutes "success"—

as well as what makes a woman "independent"—are indeed relative. "Even though I had left a good job and very pleasant associations at work, I never drove past my previous place of employment without thinking *'I'm free! I'm free!'*"[22]

Linda Burton, one of the founders of Mothers At Home, writes of another reason that some young mothers are taking a second look at the possibility of staying home full-time: the frustrating search for adequate child care. "I discovered," she writes, "to my surprise, that I missed my child when I was gone. I worried about how he was being dressed, fed, cared for. I worried that his bright inquisitiveness was being dulled by the housekeeper who, while a kind and decent person, lacked a certain intellectual vitality."

After a period of looking for an adequate commercial day care center that met her criteria, Burton tried the nanny route—with similar results. "I learned that nanny-housekeepers—no matter how good or how qualified—rarely stay around very long. A job, after all, is still a job, and even the most capable of nannies is not in the job for the long run. . . . The reality was that few modern-day nannies stuck around long enough to see a baby move into toddlerhood. Even the most congenial and affluent of employers, who gave their nannies multiple gifts, lavish vacations, free cars, high wages, and desirable working conditions, frequently complained about the eternal search for 'yet another' nanny." Finally, Burton came to realize that there was no substitute for her own care:

> My carefully worded advertisements for child care literally came back to haunt me. I was looking for someone "loving, tender, reliable, responsible, nurturing, intelligent, and resourceful." I had wanted someone with a driver's license, good English, a sense of fun, and an alert, lively manner, I wanted someone who would encourage my children's creativity, take them on interesting outings, answer all their little questions, and rock them to sleep. I wanted someone who would be a "part of the family." Slowly, painfully, after really thinking about what I wanted for

my children and rewriting advertisement after advertisement, I came to the stunning realization that the person I was looking for was right under my nose. I had been desperately trying to hire me.[23]

Many mothers are also discovering that, when all is said and done, the second income of a working mother does not amount to much when day care and other expenses are factored in. In *Welcome Home*, the monthly publication of Mothers At Home, Betty Walter estimates that most of the extra income evaporates when one considers all the costs associated with the decision of a mother to go back to work immediately. "Consider a mother who provides $15,000 per year or $1,250 per month in income to her family. Child care expenses ($400-600 per month), commuting and parking expenses ($50-100 per month), higher federal, state and local taxes ($375-425 per month), the costs of purchasing and maintaining a wardrobe of work clothes ($50-75 per month), transportation for the child ($10-20 per month), and convenience foods and meals out for lunch and dinner ($20-30 per month). In this example, these work-related expenses leave between zero and $345 extra per month, hardly a great economic bonanza."[24] Jonathan Pond of Financial Planning Information in Boston and author of *The New Century Family Money Book* points out that many stressed dual-income families often do not realize how little they benefit from a second income when all the extra expenses are added up. "A lot of couples are really shocked once they look at how much the second paycheck really brings to the family, given the hectic lifestyle they have to lead to keep two jobs."[25]

Ultimately, though, many young mothers decide to return to work—despite the paltry financial benefits—for fear that they are wasting their potential on homemaking and childrearing, while their professional talents lie fallow. In hearings before the House Select Committee on Children, Youth, and the Family, Linda Burton, the cofounder of Mothers At Home, spoke about the roots of this prevalent attitude: "More subtle than economic pressures to work, but possibly more of an influence on the state of child care in the nation, is the social pressure mothers feel. In the past twenty years, we have fostered a generation of young people who have heard nothing but put-downs about child-rearing. They have been massively encouraged to 'do something more important' with their lives. Mothering has no prestige. While we as a nation continue to respect motherhood, we have little respect for our mothers."[26]

Perhaps the single most compelling reason for returning to the workforce in the minds of many young mothers is the worry that their education would be going to waste if they were to devote full time to family concerns. This fear is reinforced by the constant reiteration of that notion in the popular media, in the universities, and in the workplace itself. By the time they marry and consider starting a family, many young women are already far along the path of preparation for a full-time career, often having embarked on a course of academic studies and professional training specifically designed to prepare them for a career in the paid workforce. Wouldn't it waste their investment of time, energy, and money in their education to forgo monetary remuneration in favor of uncompensated motherhood and housework?

Again, the answer to this question would seem to depend on the cultural status accorded these domestic activities so essential to the health and vitality of the American family. If one considers that there can be no more important task—for society or for families—than forming the hearts and minds of human beings at the age at which they are most able to be formed, no preparation could be wasted. Since it is likely that most women will continue to work outside the home both before they begin a family and after their children have grown, they will surely find professional preparation both useful and necessary; and anyone who believes that a higher education is not advantageous for one who takes on the primary burden of childrearing is simply ignorant of what forming young children entails. In fact,

when the so-called cult of domesticity was at its height in this country, American mothers were better educated than their peers in any
other country. "Despite the ideology of domesticity," writes feminist
historian Theda Skocpol, "the United States led the world in offering
higher education to women in its decentralized and fast-growing system of colleges and universities." In 1920, women already constituted
almost half of all American students in institutions of higher learning, with some 283,000 enrolled.[27]   Clearly, there is no necessary contradiction between education and domesticity.

What does stand opposed to a restoration of the status of the
housewife and mother is the ideology that demands that the two sexes
must be educated identically and with one aim: preparation for a lifetime in the professional workforce. Here again, it is—surprisingly—
feminists that have been most forthright in pointing out the
deficiencies of a purely gender-neutral system of higher education
that acknowledges no distinctions between men and women. While
only eighty-four women's colleges survive nationwide (there were
almost three hundred in 1960), enrollment is on the upswing.[28]   The
most ardent promoters of single-sex education today are feminists,
who see women's colleges as a way of giving young women the personal attention and conducive environment they need to develop their
intellectual potential, without the distractions of having to compete
and socialize with young men.

SIGNS OF HOPE

Some young mothers do seem to be realizing that the challenges and
demands of childrearing require both a more constant presence and
a significant amount of intellectual preparation. Consider the phenomenal growth of the home schooling movement. There is today a
large and highly organized constituency behind home schooling—a
constituency that did not exist even fifteen years ago. As recently as
1978, the number of children in grades kindergarten through twelve

receiving home schooling was estimated to be between ten thousand and fifteen thousand; today, even conservative estimates put the number above five hundred thousand, with advocates claiming a figure closer to a million.[29] Significantly, the surge in home schooling came during a period when public-school enrollment was declining, and most observers predict that the growing numbers of home schoolers will continue to swell.

Home schooling has become popular for a wide variety of reasons, but most people involved in the movement believe that organized government schools have failed in key areas. Concerns about violence, lack of discipline, and content of curricula are common, as is the notion that specific needs can be better met in the personal setting of the home.

Home schooling has remained something of a secret outside of the relatively small group of committed practitioners. Perhaps this is one reason that legislators in Washington, D.C. were shocked by the strength and efficacy of the home-schooling constituency five years ago when an attempt was made to impose stricter regulations on home schooling. For seven straight days in February of 1994, Capitol Hill was inundated with what many members of Congress described as the highest volume of calls, telegrams, and faxes they had ever received on a single issue. Many offices simply unplugged the phones or shut down altogether, unable to handle the flood of calls.[30]

What provoked this wave of public sentiment was an obscure, last-minute amendment to the 1994 education bill requiring every teacher in a "nonprofit" school to be certified in each subject. Tens of thousands of incensed parents around the nation saw this as a deliberate effort to quash home schooling by forcing parents to meet education bureaucracy standards in order to have the right to teach their own children, and after they had spoken, the certification language was removed from the bill by an almost unanimous vote.[31]

The interesting thing is that, for a constituency with such political clout, the home-schooling movement cannot be characterized as having a definite political tint. While it is commonly viewed as an outgrowth of the "religious right," the modern phenomenon of parents seizing direct control of their children's education actually originated at the leftmost end of the socioreligious spectrum. Unsatisfied with conventional schools because of their tendency to reinforce what they viewed as cultural and class prejudices, counterculture advocates of the New Left set up alternative schools in their homes in the late 1960s. Though few, these experiments contributed considerably to the emergence of home schooling as a social force. Those early advocates of home schooling have been followed in subsequent decades by people who gave other reasons for "dropping out" of the system.[32]

In the 1970s, Christians—primarily fundamentalists—began to home school their children to counter the secular values they believed were being promoted in the public schools. In the 1980s, home-schooling was undertaken by Catholics and also by professional parents with no particular religious beliefs. Despite the fact that home schooling is considered more mainstream today than it was twenty-five years ago, it retains a countercultural tint. Yet this may be fading thanks to the soaring number of practitioners and to some impressive results: in the largest nationwide study to date, home-schooled children averaged between the eightieth and eighty-seventh percentile in standardized achievement tests in all subject areas. At top universities, the generally positive experiences with students who have been home schooled are reassuring administrators who once harbored doubts about the capabilities of such students.[33]

While religiously-based objections to public school curricula have helped the growth of home schooling, the significance of such objections is often overemphasized; much of the revolt has to do with questions of academic quality.[34] Often, parents who began to teach their kids at home for religious reasons have been impressed by improvements in their children's behavior and academic performance.

Critics of home schooling often cite the problem of "socialization." They fear that lack of contact with other children in a normal school setting will inhibit the development of a young person. Home schooling advocates respond by citing the family networks of home schoolers that have sprung up to ensure that children have the opportunity to interact with others of their own age, in activities ranging from organized outings to cultural events to league sports. Even Ivy League university admissions officers admit that their experiences with the products of home schooling have been quite positive and that their initial fears about retarded social development were overblown. What, after all, is "socialization"? The insular and corrosive "youth culture" that is at least partly to blame for the profoundly unsettling spate of violence in the public schools compels one to turn the question back on the critics. Isn't the larger type of "socialization"—in which children learn to deal with those of many ages, especially adults—more important than finding a "clique" in school?

Until relatively recently, parents who wanted to teach their children at home faced a more formidable barrier than social stigma: state law. In the past fifteen years, however, the legal climate has become more favorable. Most of the barriers have fallen thanks to the work of home-school proponents; now home schooling is legal in all fifty states, and only a few states have restrictive laws of any type. Ironically, the success of the movement to fight state regulations is based on constitutional precedents that might have been overturned long ago were it not for certain political factors. The only reason that court challenges to home schooling did not prevail is that limiting home-schooling would have required reversing a series of Supreme Court decisions from the 1920s—decisions that have become the foundation of the modern "right to privacy." The fact that privacy rights form the basis of subsequent rulings such as *Roe vs. Wade* has so far prevented a direct attack on parents' right to educate in the home.[35]

Massive and monopolistic though it may be, public education as we know it today is in fact an innovation, having begun in the latter part of the nineteenth century. Until the 1920s there were no compulsory attendance laws, no standardized tests, no state oversight, and the evidence suggests that children actually had higher literacy rates before school attendance became mandatory. Allan Carlson has documented the hostility to family and parental influence that marked the public-school movement from its beginnings; he also notes a direct correlation between public school attendance and smaller family size, concluding that "we can indict, with justice, state education as a *direct* cause of family decline."[36]

Carlson makes the point that promoters of "progress" and state control of children—from Charlotte Perkins Gilman in the 1890s to futurist Alvin Toffler in the 1990s—have hailed the family's "loss of functions" and have preached that the passing of the domestic economy of home production of goods to industry (with its consequent weakening of family bonds) is equivalent to social progress. "Home education," Carlson writes, "viewed in this context, represents the return of a central function to the family."[37] Aside from higher academic performance, other indications that home education is already having a reinvigorating effect on families that attempt the process include a larger-than-average family size for home schoolers (3.43 children per family compared to less than two for the national average) and a reduced incidence of high-risk behavior (such as the use of illegal drugs and promiscuous sex) by children schooled at home. The higher fertility rate of home-schooling mothers could be explained by the fact that the economic benefit of maintaining one parent as a teacher in the home increases with every child.[38]

While not every mother has the capacity—or inclination—to take on the daunting project of providing a formal education to young children, the rapid growth of home schooling in recent years seems to indicate that the market for mothers ready and able to home educate is by no means saturated. Another area of growing domestic activity that may indicate a incipient renewal of home life is the homework movement. Many feminists have criticized home-based paid employment on the grounds that it leaves wives and mothers more vulnerable to "oppressive labor practices." They mean that these women would be less fulfilled and happy than their counterparts in the office, because at home they must work while handling child-rearing and domestic chores. A study by Hilary Silver of Brown University, however, shows the opposite: mothers who do paid work at home "report significantly less job-family interference than those working outside the home" and "perceive fewer tensions between their dual roles" as employee and family member.[39] Although most employers still resist the idea of so-called "telecommuting," the total number of workers performing some or all of their work from home seems to have grown over the last decade. And contrary to the preconceptions of most employers, working at home actually seems to increase productivity among most workers, anywhere from 20 to 40 percent according to some studies.[40] The major obstacles to further expansion of this promising option for mothers are not so much related to costs or to productivity as to administrative habits, because the business school products who are managers of most corporations remain behind the technology curve in their dealings with employees.

Any restoration of a sane domestic equilibrium will also require a wholesale reconceiving of work in our culture. "If our job is riding us, and not vice versa," writes author and educator Dennis Helming, "there's no conceivable way that we can make it into something more than an obsessive chase after labor's fruits and rewards (money, power, fame), draining the job of any intrinsic value.... Frenzied work tends to metastasize more and more, with all the ensuing familiar ravages (personal, familial, social)."[41] Yet Helming's characterization seems a spot-on description of an all-too-common problem of American workers: rampant activism with no time allowed for studied reflection, which results in both professional burn-out and an impoverished home life. For the majority of workers who are not in a position to set the tone of an entire office, to put work in its proper perspective and to give home its due may mean scaling back. They may need to make the difficult decision to sacrifice some measure of professional success, status, or advancement for the sake of the family. Doubtless, the economic sacrifice entailed can itself have detrimental effects on family life, but for mothers and fathers who view the quality of family life as the primary motive for their devotion to professional work, it could be a step in the right direction.

Ultimately, a reformation of cultural attitudes about work and its relation to domestic life must be based on an understanding of work as self-gift—giving of one's energy and talents for the sake of others, particularly one's family. Any significant change in our cultural attitudes implies a change in our "belief systems"—what Richard Gill calls our "sense of personal limits, self-restraint, even occasionally self-sacrifice." It therefore makes perfect sense that the level of parents' religious commitment would have a substantial effect on their view of work, the health of their families, and the vitality of their domestic life. Sociological studies show a clear link between a high level of religious commitment and improved physical and mental health, lower rates of divorce, higher marital satisfaction, larger family size—in short, just about every objective measure of domestic vitality. Most interesting, there seems to be a clear statistical correlation between families with a high level of religious commitment and families in which the mother is at home during the children's formative years. Strong families are based on each member's giving to the others unconditionally; sociological data now seem to confirm the commonsense notion that religious practice is a primary factor in such selfless behavior.[42]

Selfless sacrifice for others, even in the context of the family, is undermined by the ideology of radical individualism that permeates modern American life. But even here, there are signs that we are, as a result of our advanced state of social and familial decay, prepared to question our dominant philosophy of individualism. More and more, it seems, Americans are concluding that our major ideologies are not organized along radically different philosophical lines. While there are indeed serious differences in emphasis and theory, the fact is that both liberalism and conservatism as we know them in this country are, in essence, political philosophies that exalt radical individualism—albeit in distinct ways. Modern liberalism holds that the primary value which society—and government—must uphold is the right of the individual to think, speak, and behave in the way that he deems best, so long as his behavior does not interfere directly with the freedom of others. This exaltation of individual rights essentially denies the right and duty of the community to regulate and protect itself in a democratic fashion by outlawing or otherwise discouraging behavior that it deems harmful to the common good or destructive of society and its institutions. The continuing disintegration of the family and other manifestations of social chaos are leading many—even on the Left—to question traditional liberal dogma about the absolute primacy of the individual in the realm of moral choices, particularly those proved to have detrimental consequences for the community.

Modern conservatism holds that the primary value which society—and government—must uphold is the right of unrestricted economic activity in a "free market" without government interference. This exaltation of the unrestricted use of capital denies the right and duty of the community to regulate economic transactions in the interest of the common good, toward which the economy is ostensibly oriented. This conservatism also lacks a principle on which the community can protect the property, capital, and economic independence of families when those family goods are threatened by "market forces"—even if those forces consist of large and powerful business interests bent on destroying smaller competitors, tightening their grip on a specific market, or enriching the management of a company at the expense of the company's own workers and the national or local economy. The self-interested and anti-social behavior of corporate chieftains who are more loyal to their own bottom line than their community, their workers, or their country, has led to a reexamination of some of the laissez-faire doctrines and to a new willingness to limit corporate power if that is what is required to provide a measure of economic independence and security to the nonmanagerial class.

While American liberals and conservatives are thus the two sides of the one coin of radical individualism, both ideologies do acknowledge a point at which the rights of the community take precedence over those of the individual. For some liberals, that point is reached when they perceive that the workings of the free market are substantially inequitable; for some conservatives, when individual behavior can be shown to be detrimental to the moral tone or the moral well-being of the community. But the criteria for overriding individual autonomy are inconsistent in both cases and based more on ideological predilection than on a coherent political or social philosophy. And when it comes to enacting policy, individualism tends to prevail almost by default, since the radical right of the individual to do as he wishes is a social philosophy that can be easily grasped, however simplistic it may be.

For those who feel, however inchoately, that the radical individualism at the core of both major political philosophies presents an almost insuperable barrier to the enactment of sane family and social policy on the one hand, and sane economic policy on the other, I suggest a new paradigm. In answer to the heresy of conservative individualism, we must clearly enunciate the principles of a new economy ordered toward the good of our citizens rather than toward merely abstract goods like growth, efficiency, profit, and productivity. As elements of an economy that serves the interests of real people, real families, and real communities, those concepts have value; if they simply dictate a bottom-line approach to economics that views persons as a means toward achieving some unspecified and perpetual goal of directionless economic expansion, they are worse than useless; they are positively dangerous. The economy exists for man, not man for the economy—a fundamental idea often ignored in discussions of economy which tend to revolve around the almost mystical concept of "growth."

One might think that this rather obvious principle would be easily understood and readily agreed to by those who call themselves "conservative." The truth is that most American conservatives adhere to the view that government ought not to favor any particular social arrangement over any other because such a preference might sustain inefficiencies that would be weeded out in a naturally predatory economic environment. Hence the continuing resistance by a considerable body of those on the right to implementing pro-family tax proposals, such as increasing the individual deduction for children or giving a child tax credit to heads of households. It is a common laissez-faire objection that any preference in the tax code for traditional family arrangements over nontraditional would be an unwarranted government intrusion into the economy. This speaks volumes about the doctrinaire rigidity that prevents conservatives from doing anything effective to ease the enormous tax burden on families and that even blinds them to the fact that a predatory capitalism based on creating new needs will promote social chaos.

It is not enough, as some conservatives suggest, to eliminate the subsidies that government now provides for destructive behavior such as illegitimacy and abortion. In matters of economic and tax policy, the choice is clear: We either favor the family or we favor the forces that are working for its destruction. To take just one example, if we decide that our society has an interest in making it possible for mothers to stay at home with their pre-school children, rather than letting them be forced by financial necessity into the workplace, it is perfectly rational to institute a preference for that option—temporary or otherwise—into the tax code. We cannot blindly hope in the mysterious working of the market's "invisible hand" to produce that result—especially when that hand has already pushed many mothers into the workforce against their will.

Strengthening families has vast implications for our conception of social welfare as well. Unaided by strong families, neither the market nor government will go very far in meeting the needs of the less fortunate members of society, no matter how "enlightened" the policy approach. In order to meet those needs where they should be met—in the context of the community—we will have to dispense with one of the more destructive notions of our age: namely, the strict doctrine of separation of church and state which has been artificially inserted into our constitutional tradition by those with an explicitly secularist agenda. The idea that we should take charity out of the hands of locally-based organizations and individuals, who often are motivated to help the less fortunate by a religiously inspired love of God and their fellow man, and give it to a faceless federal welfare bureaucracy motivated by self-perpetuation is ludicrous and has been thoroughly discredited by our experience with federally controlled and administered welfare. Individuals who generously use their time and talents to aid the less fortunate will usually come from healthy families, and it follows that the best thing that governments can do in the long term to perpetuate private charity is to follow policy pre-scriptions that have the aim of strengthening the family.

The liberal ideal that a benign federal welfare state will help the disadvantaged has failed, and its failure has its roots in the welfare system's own contribution to the disintegration of homes and fami-lies. But simply handing the responsibility for welfare over to state governments will do nothing to address the spiritual impoverishment that we persist in calling poverty. Organized religion can ameliorate that spiritual poverty while at the same time effectively ministering to the resultant material devastation. If, as a society, we come to rec-ognize once again the unique and foundational role that religious in-stitutions play in providing the moral norms upon which the maintenance of families, homes, and communities depend, it is rea-sonable—indeed necessary—for society to promote the private sup-port of these institutions and their activities as much as possible. The dismantling of the current government welfare structure must be ac-companied by more tax incentives to encourage private generosity to religious institutions with a mission to improve the spiritual and material lot of the underprivileged. Our experience with welfare illustrates the point, made repeatedly in these pages, that the essence of a home includes much more than material shelter; it also entails the nonmaterial environment of self-giving in which families and individuals thrive.

If we see the flight from domesticity as something harmful for society and harmful for families—as a malady that needs to be arrested—then we will have to revise the way we look at both work and home. We will have to bring to our conception of work more of the spirit of service and inconspicuous dedication, more of the willingness to perform "menial," unglamorous, hidden tasks for the sake of others—particularly family—that has traditionally characterized the work of mothers and homemakers. At the same time, we will have to accord to homemaking and child rearing more of the status, cultural recognition, professionalism, preparation, and dedication now almost exclusively associated with the workplace. Only through acknowledging the complementarity of work outside of the home and work in the home—and the dependence of the former sphere on the latter—can we hope to arrive at equity and due deference for the true heroes and heroines of our society: men and women for whom family comes first. Only by producing strong families can we hope to make any progress in dealing with our various—and all too numerous—social ills.

Notes

Introduction

1 F. J. Sheed, *Society and Sanity* (London: Sheed and Ward, 1953).

2 Elizabeth Harvey, "Short-Term and Long-Term Effects of Early Parental Employment on Children of the National Longitudinal Survey of Youth," *Developmental Psychology* (March 1999): 445-59.

3 "Good News for Moms: No One Misses You," *Vital STATS: The Numbers Behind the News*, Newsletter of the Statistical Assessment Service (March 1999): 1.

4 Barbara Vobejda, "Mothers' Employment Works for Children: Study Finds No Long-Term Damage," *Washington Post* (March 1, 1999): A1.

5 Dolores Kong, "Study says working mothers don't cause children harm," *Boston Globe,* (March 1, 1999): A1.

6 Paul Recer, "Working Moms Not Shortchanging Kids, Study Suggests," *Atlanta Journal and Constitution* (March 1, 1999): A1.

7 "Good News for Moms," *Vital STATS*: 1.

8 Ibid.

9 Ibid.

10 Diane Fisher, "When Science Serves Politics," *Investor's Business Daily* (March 5, 1999): Viewpoint.

11 "Good News for Moms," *Vital STATS*.

12 Fisher, "When Science Serves Politics."

13 Danielle Crittenden, "Day-Care Delusions," *The Weekly Standard* (March 22, 1999): 16.

14 Remarks by President Clinton in Commencement Address to Grambling State University Graduates, Eddie Robinson Stadium, Grambling, Louisiana, May 23, 1999.

15 See "Affordable Child Care, Education, Security, and Safety Act," introduced into 106th Congress by the Clinton Administration, and "Working Families Flexibility Act of 1999," introduced into the same session with the backing of the Republican leadership.

1   The Real Child Care Crisis

1 Lee Rainwater, *The Moynihan Report and the Politics of Controversy; a Transaction Social Science and Public Policy Report* (Cambridge: MIT Press, 1967).

2 Paul Galloway, "Moynihan/New York Senator Recalls Triumph, Turmoil Surrounding His Prophetic 'Sissors' Report," *Houston Chronicle* (September 9, 1986): Lifestyle, 3.

3 David Popenoe, *Disturbing the Nest: Family Change and Decline in Modern Societies* (New York: A. de Gruyter, 1988).

4 Barbara Dafoe Whitehead, "Dan Quayle Was Right," *Atlantic Monthly* (April 1993): 47-81.

5 Lisa Schiffren, "It Seems Dan Quayle Had It Right After All," *Houston Chronicle* (June 14, 1998): Outlook, 4.

6 Brian Robertson, "In Academia, New Praise for the Nuclear Family," *Insight* (March 14, 1994): 18-20.

7 Stephanie Coontz, *The Way We Never Were: American Families and the Nostalgia Trap* (New York: Basic Books, 1992).

8 Whitehead, "Dan Quayle."

9 Arlie Russel Hochschild, *The Time Bind: When Work Becomes Home and Home Becomes Work* (New York: Metropolitan Books, 1997); also Richard T. Gill, *Posterity Lost: Progress, Ideology, and the Decline of the Amerian Family* (Lanham, Md.: Rowman & Littlefield Publishers, 1997), 31.

10 Gill, *Posterity Lost*, 32.

11 Ibid., 239.

12 Ibid., 35-45.

13 F. Carolyn Graglia, *Domestic Tranquillity: A Brief Against Feminism* (Dallas: Spence Publishing, 1998), 291.

14 Jacqueline F. de Gaston, Larry Jensen, and Stan Weed, "A Closer Look at Adolescent Sexual Activity," *Journal of Youth and Adolescence* 24 (1995): 465-78.

15 Graglia, *Domestic Tranquillity*, 301-2.

16 Elizabeth M. Aldeman and Stanford B. Friedman, "Behavioral Problems of Affluent Youth," *Pediatric Annals* 24 (1994): 186-91.

17 Mark Warr, "Parents, Peers, and Delinquency," *Social Forces* 72 (1993): 247-64.

18 Joel Paris and Hallie Frank, "Perceptions of Parental Bonding in Borderline Patients," *American Journal of Psychiatry* 146 (1989): 1498-99.

19 American Academy of Pediatrics, Committee on Communications, "Children, Adolescents, and Television," *Pediatrics* 85 (1990): 1119.

20 Gill, *Posterity Lost*, 36.

21 Barbara Vobejda, "Love Conquers What Ails Teens, Study Finds," *Washington Post* (September 10, 1997): A1.

22 Cal Thomas, "Kids Are Tuned In to Reality," *The Dayton Daily News* (March 3, 1995): 11A.

23 Peter L. Benson, *The Troubled Journey: A Portrait of 6th-12th Grade Youth* (Minneapolis: Search Institute, 1993), 84.

24 "What Mothers Want Today and Every Day; Actually, Both Men and Women Would Like More Family Time," *Los Angeles Times* (May 14, 1995): M4.

25 U.S. Bureau of Labor Statistics (published tabulations).

26 Ibid.

27 Ibid.

28 Ibid.

29 Ibid.

30 Ibid.

31 William T. Bailey, "Fathers Involvement in Responding to Infants: 'More' May Not Be 'Better,'" *Psychological Reports* 74 (1994): 92-94.

32 William R. Mattox, Jr., "Men At Work: Crafting Employment Policies to Facilitate Fathering," *Insight* (June 1993): 1.

33 "Families and the Labor Market, 1969-1999: Analyzing the 'Time Crunch'," A Report by the Council of Economic Advisors (May, 1999): 13.

34 Robert Rector, "Facts About American Families and Day Care," The Heritage Foundation's *FYI #170* (January 23, 1998): 1.

35 Bureau of Labor Statistics, (published tabulations).

36 Ibid.

37 Rector, "American Families."

38 U.S. Bureau of the Census, (published tabulations).

39 Ibid.

40 Karl Zinsmeister, "Why Encouraging Day Care Is Unwise," *The American Enterprise* 9:3 (May/June 1998): 4-7.

41 Ibid., 5.

42 Ibid.

43 John Bowlby, *A Secure Base: Parent-Child Attachment and Healthy Human Development* (New York: Basic Books, 1988).

44 Margaret Talbot, "Attachment Theory: The Ultimate Experiment," *The New York Times Magazine* (May 24, 1998): 28; also D. W. Winnicott, *The Family and Individual Development* (London: Tavistock Publications, 1966).

45 Karl Zinsmeister, "The Importance of Early Childhood Attachment," *The American Enterprise* 9:3, (May/June 1998): 30.

46 Talbot, "Attachment Theory," 27.

47 Zinsmeister, "Importance," 30-31.

48 Ibid., 32.

49 Ibid., 30.

50 Talbot, "Attachment Theory."

51 Ibid., 30.

52 Ibid.

53 Ibid.

54 Zinsmeister, "Why Encouraging Day Care ," 4.

55 Maggie Gallagher, *Enemies of Eros* (Washington, DC: Regnery, 1996), 78.

56 Karl Zinsmeister, "The Problem With Day Care," *The American Enterprise* 9:3 (May/June 1998): 30-31.

57 Ibid., 32.

58 Ibid.

59 "New Research," *The Family in America*, newsletter of the Howard Institute (January 1991).

60 Sonalde Desai, P. Lindsay Chase-Landsdale, Robert T. Michael, "Mother or Market? Effects of Maternal Employment on the Intellectual Ability of 4-year-old Children," *Demography* 26 (1989): 545-61.

61 "New Research," *The Family in America* (October 1995).

62 Jude Cassidy and Lisa J. Berlin, "The Insecure/Ambivalent Pattern of Attachment: Theory and Research," *Child Development* 65 (1994): 971-91.

63 G. K. Chesterton, *What's Wrong With the World* (San Francisco: Ignatius Press, 1994).

64 Anne S. Johansen, et al., "Child Care and Children's Illness," *American Journal of Public Health* 78:9 (September 1988): 1175-77.

65 Cynthia R. Howard and Michael Weitzman, "Breast or Bottle: Practical Aspects of Infant Nutrition in the First Six Months," *Pediatric Annals* 21 (1992): 619-31.

66 Alan S. Ryan, et al., "Recent Declines in Breast-feeding in the United States, 1984-1989," *Pediatrics* 88 (1991): 719-27.

67 "New Research," *The Family in America* (July 1995).

68 Zinsmeister, "Problem With Day Care," 34-35.

69 Ibid., 34.

70 "Americans Believe Mom is Best Child Care Provider," Family Research Council's *In Focus* (1998).

71 Steven A. Capps, "Reiner Convenes Panel on Child Development," *The Orange County Register* (March 26, 1999): B7.

2 The Vanishing Homestead

1 Suzanne M. Bianchi and Daphne Spain, *Balancing Act: Motherhood, Marriage, and Employment Among American Women* (New York: Russel Sage Foundation, 1996), 5.

2 Ibid., 4-23.

3 Allan Carlson, "The Peril of Statistics: Pregnant Teenagers and the Retreat from Marriage," *The Family in America* (July 1999): 3-4.

4 Ibid., 1-2.

5 Bianchi and Spain, *Balancing Act*, 196.

6 "New Research," *The Family in America* (October 1992).

7 "Hourly Wage Decile Cutoffs, for All Workers, from the CPS ORG, 1973-1998 (1998 Dollars), Economic Policy Institute analyis of U.S. Bureau of the Census Current Population Survey data.

8 Bianchi and Spain, *Balancing Act*, 15.

9 John P. Markum, "Explaining Protestant Fertility: Belief, Commitment, and Homogamy," *The Sociological Quarterly* 27:4 (Winter 1986): 547-55.

10 See Charmaine Crouse Yoest, "Behind the Push for Day Care ... Parents At Home: Still the Silent Majority, *Family Policy* (March 1998): 1-15.

11 Robert J. Samuelson, "The Two-Earner Myth," *Washington Post* (January 22, 1997): A23.

12 Robert D. Mare, "Five Decades of Educational Assortative Mating," *American Sociological Review* 56 (1991): 15-32; Deborah A. Stiles, Judith L. Gibbons, and Jo De la Garza Schnellman, "Opposite Sex Ideal in the U.S.A. and Mexico as Perceived by Young Adolescents," *Journal of Cross-Cultural Psychology* 21 (1990): 180-99.

13 Lloyd Grove "The Limited Life of a Political Wife; For the Spouse, Avoiding Conflict May Be the Top Job," *Washington Post* (March 19, 1992): C1.

14 Helen Gurley Brown, *Sex and the Single Girl* (New York: Pocket Books, 1965), quoted in Jessie Bernard, *The Future of Marriage* (New York: Dial Press, 1974), 226.

15 Melissa B. Robinson, "Franks slams Dodd for comment on stay-at-home moms," *Associated Press*, (February 26, 1998).

16 U.S. Bureau of the Census (published statistics).

17 Ibid.

18 Alexis de Tocqueville, *Democracy in America*, Lawrence A. Cremin ed. (Richmond: William Byrd Press, 1965): vii.

19 Catherine Beecher, *An Essay on the Education of Female Teachers* (1835), in *The Educated Woman in America*, ed. Barbara M. Cross (New York: Teachers College Press, 1965): 82.

20 Ibid., 83.

21 Elizabeth Cady Stanton, *Eighty Years and More* (New, York: Schocken Books, 1971), 112-13.

22 Theda Skocpol, *Protecting Soldiers and Mothers: The Political Origins of Social Policy in the United States* (Cambridge: Harvard University Press, 1992), 432-35.

23 Ibid.

24 Ibid., 333.

25 Harry Overstreet, *Where Children Come First: A Study of the P.T.A. Idea* (Chicago, National Congress of Parents and Teachers, 1949), 194.

26 Molly Ladd-Taylor, *Mother-Work: Women, Child Welfare, and the State, 1890-1930* (Chicago: University of Illinois Press, 1994), 50.

27 Ibid., 45-47.

28 Skocpol, *Protecting Soldiers and Mothers*, 448-52.

29 Ibid., 337.

30 Alexandra Towle, *Mothers: A Celebration in Prose, Poetry, and Photographs of Mothers and Motherhood* (New York: Simon and Schuster, 1988), 27-28.

31 Skocpol, *Protectin Soldiers and Mothers*, 336.

32 Ibid., 424-32.

33 Ibid., 425.

34 Ibid.

35 Ibid., 430.

36 Ibid., 432.

37 Ibid., 452.

38 Ibid., 466-67.

39 Ibid., 468.

40 Ibid., 483.

41 Ibid., 481.

42 Ladd-Taylor, *Mother-Work*, 80.

43 Skocpol, *Protecting Soldiers and Mothers*, 500.

44 Ibid., 504.

45 Robyn Muncy, *Creating a Female Dominion in American Reform,* *1890-1935* (New York: Oxford University Press, 1991), 162.

46 Skocpol, *Soldiers and Mothers,* 373-74.

47 Ibid., 377-82.

48 Ibid., 380.

49 Ibid., 393-411.

50 Ibid., 420.

51 Ibid., 408.

52 Ladd-Taylor, *Mother-Work,* 106.

53 Ibid., 107.

54 Ibid., 113.

55 Ibid.

56 Ibid., 118.

57 Sheila M. Rothman, *Woman's Proper Place,* (New York: Basic Books, 1978), 157.

58 Ibid., 162.

59 Ladd-Taylor, *Mother-Work,* 118.

60 Ibid., 140.

61 *Charlotte Perkins Gilman: A Non-Fiction Reader,* ed. Larry Ceplair (New York: Columbia University Press, 1991): 16-17.

62 Ibid., 17.

63 Ibid., 18.

64 Ibid., 19-20.

65 Ibid., 36-38.

66 Ibid., 135.

67 Ibid., 200.

68 Ibid., 247.

69 Ibid., 107-25

70 Ladd-Taylor, *Mother-Work,* 111.

71 Ceplair, *Gilman: Non-Fiction Reader,* 36, 104.

72 Ibid., 58.

73 Ibid., 239.

74 Ladd-Taylor, *Mother-Work,* 113-15.

75 Ceplair, *Gilman: Non-Fiction Reader,* 240.

76 Rothman, *Woman's Proper Place,* 160.

77 Ceplair, *Gilman: Non-Fiction Reader,* 275.

78 Ibid., 276.

79 Ladd-Taylor, *Mother-Work*, 198.

80 Ibid., 199.

81 Skocpol, *Protecting Soldiers and Mothers*, 408.

82 Graglia, *Domestic Tranquillity*, 105.

83 Allan C. Carlson, *From Cottage to Work Station: The Family's Search for Social Harmony in the Industrial Age* (San Francisco: Ignatius Press, 1993), 159.

84 National Manpower Council, *Work in the Lives of Married Women; Proceedings of a Conference on Womanpower held October 20-25, 1957, at Arden House, Harriman Campus of Columbia University* (New York: Columbia University Press, 1958), 145.

85 Ibid., 172, 201.

86 Jessie Bernard, *The Future of Motherhood* (New York: Dial Press, 1974), 268.

87 Jane J. Mansbridge, *Why We Lost the ERA* (Chicago: University of Chicago Press, 1986), 99.

88 Ibid., 103.

89 Graglia, *Domestic Tranquillity*, 126.

90 Ibid., 146.

91 Mansbridge, *Why We Lost the ERA*, 100.

92 Graglia, *Domestic Tranquillity*, 3.

93 Ibid., 138.

94 Ladd-Taylor, *Mother-Work*, 6.

95 Ibid., 5.

96 Ibid., 31.

97 Hochschild, *Time Bind*.

98 Ibid., 243.

3 *Fleeing the Haven for the Heartless World*

1 Mansbridge, *Why We Lost the ERA*, 106.

2 Bureau of Labor Statistics (published tabulations).

3 Lonnie Golden, "Working Time in the United States—Trends, Influences and Prospects," *WSI-Mitteilungen: Working Time Reduction in Europe: Discussions—Actions—Obstacles* (1998); see also Juliet Schor, *The Overworked American: the Unexpected Decline of Leisure* (New York: Ba-

sic Books, 1991) and Shelley Donald Coolidge, "9 to 5 and then some, and then some, and then some . . .," *Christian Science Monitor* (May 24, 1999): A1.

4 Hochschild, *Time Bind*, 9.

5 Carlson, *From Cottage to Work Station*, p. 167; see also A Report by the Council of Economic Advisers, "Families and the Labor Market, 1969-1999: Analyzing the "Time Crunch" (May 1999), 13.

6 Golden, "Working Time."

7 Robert Wuthnow, *Poor Richard's Principle* (Princeton: Princeton University Press, 1996), 21.

8 Anna Quindlen, "Men at Work," *The New York Times* (February 18, 1990), op-ed.

9 Hochschild, *Time Bind*, 13.

10 Ibid., 214.

11

12 Richard Harwood, "More Credit Than Credit Is Due?" *Washington Post* (May 11, 1998): A23.

13 Hochschild, *Time Bind*, 205.

14 Wuthnow, *Poor Richard's Principle*, 86.

15 Ibid.

16 Ibid., 33.

17 Susan Jacoby, "A Good Day in Any Age," *The New York Times Magazine* (June 17, 1990).

18 Carlson, *From Cottage to Work Station*, 45.

19 Wuthnow, *Poor Richard's Principle*, 125.

20 Timothy Shay Arthur, *Advice to Young Men on their Duties and Conduct in Life*, (Philadelphia: Lippincott, 1850).

21 G.K. Chesterton, *All Things Considered* (London: Cox and Wyman Ltd., 1908), 70.

22 George Gilder, *Men and Marriage* (Gretna: Pelican Publishing Co., 1986), 172.

23 Ibid., 173.

24 Adriano Tilgher, *Homo Faber: Work Through the Ages* (Chicago: Henry Regnery Co., 1947), 141.

25 Gill, *Posterity Lost*, 201.

26 Ibid., 199.

27 "U.S. Savings Rate Hits Lowest Level Since 1930s," *Reuters* (November 2, 1998).

28 Gill, *Posterity Lost*, 208.

4 *Making It*

1 Author's calculations, based on published tabulations from the Bureau of the Census, 1997.

2 Ibid.

3 David A. Macpherson and Barry T. Hirsch, "Wages and Gender Composition: Why Do Women's Jobs Pay Less?" *Journal of Labor Economics* 13 (July 1995): 4-6, Table A1; also June O'Neill, "The Shrinking Pay Gap," *Wall Street Journal* (October 7, 1994).

4 Lester C. Thurow, "What Boom? Two-Thirds of U.S.A. Stuck in 1973," *USA Today* (November 11, 1998).

5 Allan C. Carlson, "Gender, Children, and Social Labor: Transcending the 'Family Wage Dilemma,'" *Journal of Social Issues* 52:3 (1996): 137-61.

6 Allan C. Carlson, "American Business and the New Politics of the Family," *The Family in America* (June 1987): 2-3.

7 Nancy Hellmich, "Never Enough Time for Women's Work," *USA Today* (May 11, 1995): 4D.

8 Chinhui Juhn, "Relative Wage Trends, Women's Work, & Family Income," *American Enterprise Institute Studies on Understanding Economic Inequality* (Washington, D.C.: AEI Press, 1996): 9.

9 Ibid.

10 Author's calculations, Bureau of the Census (published tabulations).

11 Ibid.

12 Carlson, *From Cottage to Work Station*, 84.

13 Ibid., 135.

14 Diana Furchtgott-Roth, "Working Wives Widen 'Income Gap'," *Wall Street Journal* (June 20, 1995): A18

15 Carlson, "Gender, Children, and Social Labor.

16 Carlson, "American Business and the New Politics of the Family," 2-3.

17 Carlson, "Gender, Children, and Social Labor."

18 Paul Adam Blanchard, "Insert the Word 'Sex'-How Segregationists Handed Feminists a 1964 'Civil Rights' Victory Against the Family," *The Family in America* (March 1998).

19 Ibid.

20 Ibid.

21 Ibid.

22 Carlson, "Gender, Children, and Social Labor," 147-48.

23 "A Survey of Women and Work," *Economist* (July 18, 1998): 14.

24 Bureau of the Census (published tabulations).

25 Amy Graham and Phillip J. Longman, "The Cost of Children," *U.S. News and World Report* (March 30, 1998): 50-53, 56-58.

26 Melvin L. Oliver and Thomas N. Shapiro, "Wealth of a Nation," *The American Journal of Economics and Sociology* 49 (1990): 129-151.

27 Carlson, "Gender, Children, and Social Labor," 142.

28 Bernard, *Future of Marriage,* 128.

29 James P. Mitchell in National Manpower Council, *Work in the Lives of Married Women,* 15-19.

30 U.S. Department of Education, National Center for Education Statistics, Integrated Post-Secondary Education Data Systems, "Completions" Surveys (1996).

31 "Women and Work," *Economist,* 4.

32 Brian Robertson, "A Baby's Place is In The Home," *The Human Life Review* (Fall 1990): 57.

33 "Corporate On-site Care," *The New York Times Magazine,* 41.

34 Norie Quintos Danyliw, "Got Mother's Milk?" *U.S. News and World Report* (December 15, 1997): 79.

35 David Wagner, "Turning Hearts Towards the Office," *Insight* (July 22, 1996): 2.

36 Ibid., 3.

37 Ibid., 6.

38 Geoff Dench, *The Frog, the Prince, and the Problem of Men* (London: Neanderthal, 1994).

39 Hochschild, *Time Bind,* 205.

40 Hilaire Belloc, *The Servile State,* (Indianapolis: Liberty Classics, 1977).

5 *An Outline of Sanity*

1 Robert Rector, "How to Strengthen America's Crumbling Families," *Heritage Foundation Backgrounder* no. 894 (April 28, 1992).

2 Ibid.

3 Martin J. Dannenfelser, Jr., "Tax Reform and Working Families," *At the Podium* (April 15, 1997).

4 Rector, "How to Strengthen America's Crumbling Families."

5 Gilder, *Men and Marriage*, 93.

6 Carlson, *From Cottage to Work Station*, 22.

7 See, for example, Alan Reynolds, "Rich Rewards," *National Review* (March 22, 1999).

8 "Women and Work," *The Economist*, 16.

9 Ibid.

10 Allan Carlson, "Third Ways, Middle Ways, and the Family Way," *The Family in America* (May 1997).

11 David Blankenhorn and Allan Carlson, "Marriage and Taxes," *The Weekly Standard* (February 9, 1998): 5.

12 Ibid., 26.

13 Ibid.

14 Ibid.

15 Gilder, *Men and Marriage*, 95.

16 Allan C. Carlson, *Family Questions* (New Brunswick: Transaction Publishers, 1988), 9.

17 Ibid.

18 Ibid.

19 Allan Carlson, *The Family in America* (March 1998), 3.

20 Carlson, *Cottage to Work Station*, 23.

21 William R. Mattox Jr., "Men at Work: Crafting Employment Policies to Facilitate Fathering," *Insight* (June 1993): 3.

22 Terence P. Jeffrey, "Washington Hates My Wife," *Human Events* (December 20, 1996): 7.

23 Jan Crawford Greenburg, "Lack of Quality Day Care Called 'A Silent Crisis,'" *Chicago Tribune* (October 24, 1997): 1.

24 Allan Carlson "The New Child Abuse: Two Case-Studies of Wrong Headed Public Policy," *The Family in America* (July 1998): 2.

25 Ibid.

26 Ibid., 1.

27 Ibid.

28 Maggie Gallagher and Barbara Defoe Whitehead, "End No-Fault Divorce?" *First Things* (August/September 1997): 24-30.

29 Ibid.

30 Gilder, *Men and Marriage,* 98.

31 Gallagher and Whitehead, "End No-Fault Divorce?"

32 Ibid.

33 Nadine Brozan, "Mondale Proposes Family Impact Statement," *The New York Times* (February 26, 1974): 32.

34 Ibid.

35 Carlson, *Family Questions,* 139-54.

36 Mary Ann Glendon, *Rights Talk: The Impoverishment of Political Discourse* (New York: Free Press, 1991).

37 John Mueller "Taxation," in *Natural Law and Contemporary Public Policy* (Washington, D.C.: Georgetown University Press, 1998), 219-79.

38 Ibid.

39 Ibid.

40 Ibid.

41 Ibid.

42 Ibid.

43 Ibid.

6   Striking a Balance

1 Sandra Evans, "Girls Go to Work on Their Future; Nationwide Effort Aims to Show a Woman's Place Is Everywhere," *Washington Post* (April 29, 1993): A1.

2 Julia Vitullo-Martin, "Mother's Day History," *The Baltimore Sun* (May 6, 1998): 15A.

3 *Los Angeles Times* (May 10, 1998): M4.

4 Evans, "Girls Go to Work on Their Future."

5 Katha Pollitt, "Cultivating Girl Power; Could Taking Daughters to Work Lead to Militance?" *Chicago Tribune* (May 1, 1994): 4.

6 Gill, *Posterity Lost,* 280-81.

7 Mueller, "Taxation."

8 U.S. Bureau of the Census (published statistics).

9 Jennifer Roback Morse, "Why the Market Can't Raise Our Children For Us," *The American Enterprise* (May/June 1998): 56.

10 Steve Crump, "Many Women Leave Rat Race to Become Full-Time Moms," *Portland Oregonian* (February 15, 1998): B9.

11 Ibid.

12 Morse, "Why the Market Can't Raise Our Children For Us."

13 Ibid.

14 Ibid., 57.

15 Ibid.

16 Iris Krasnow, "Discovering Motherhood," *The American Enterprise* (May/June 1998): 46.

17 Ibid., 47.

18 Ibid.

19 Judy Pasternak, "Opting for the Job of Mothering," *Los Angeles Times* (December 12, 1997): A1.

20 Ibid.

21 Ibid.

22 Linda Burton, Janet Dittmer, and Cheri Loveless,*What's a Smart Woman Like You Doing at Home?* (Vienna: Mothers At Home, 1992), 106.

23 Ibid., 46-54.

24 Betty Walter, "Is Homemaking An Affordable Choice?" Mothers at Home *Public Policy Update* (October, 1995).

25 Charles A. Jaffe, "That second income may not be worth the effort in some families," *Allentown Morning Call* (February 27, 1994): D1.

26 Burton, Dittmer, and Loveless, *What's a Smart Woman Like You Doing At Home?*, 151.

27 Skocpol, *Protecting Soldiers and Mothers*, 341.

28 Susan C. Thomson, "Women's Colleges: They're Back and Thriving," *St. Louis Post-Dispatch*, (December 1, 1994): A1.

29 Brian Robertson,"Is Home Schooling in a Class of Its Own?" *Insight* (October 17, 1994): 6-9.

30 Ibid.

31 Ibid.

32 Ibid.

33 Ibid.

34 Ibid.

35 Ibid.

36 Allan Carlson, "Will Family-Centered Education Strengthen Families?" *The Family in America* (September 1998): 4.

37 Ibid., 5-6.

38 Ibid., 6.

39 Hilary Silver, "Homework and Domestic Work," *Sociological Forum* 8 (1993): 181-202.

40 Carolin Hull, "The Flexible Workplace," *Insight* (March 1992): 3.

41 Dennis Helming, *The Examined Life: The Art of Knowing, Owning, and Giving Yourself* (Dallas: Spence Publishing Company, 1997): 156-57.

42 Allan Carlson, "Faith of Our Fathers (and Homemaking Mothers)," *The Family in America* (March 1997): 2.

Index

A NOTE ON THE AUTHOR

BRIAN C. ROBERTSON is a research fellow at the New
Economy Information Service in Washington, D.C. He
has written for *National Review*, the *Washington Times*,
World, *Chronicles*, *Crisis*, and *Human Life Review*.

This book was designed and set into type
by Mitchell S. Muncy,
with cover art by Stephen J. Ott,
and printed and bound
by Quebecor Printing Book Press
Brattleboro, Vermont.

The text face is Minion Multiple Master,
designed by Robert Slimbach
and issued in digital form by Adobe Systems,
Mountain View, California, in 1991.

The index is by IndExpert,
Fort Worth, Texas.

The paper is acid-free and is of archival quality.

23